MW01657055

Journey from Anxiety to Freedom

A Biblical Look at Finances Through the Lens of Sabbath Economics

G. Richard Truitt, Jr.
William F. Robertson

ISBN 978-1-5218-7594-0

William F. Robertson & Associates
6100 Western Place, Suite 912
Fort Worth, TX 76107
817.870.1242
800.972.6790
www.wfrplanning.com

All biblical quotations (unless otherwise noted) are taken from the **English Standard Version** Bible.

Dedication

◆ ◆ ◆

To my three girls, Janie, Sally, and Katie,
and wonderful wife Karen.

We are anxious about the future; a product of our materialistic culture. Yet, God has promised to care for us as he cares for the birds and the lilies of the field. We live in tension as we increasingly attempt to live the life that God has promised.

Table of Contents

Preface

◆ ◆ ◆

One of the enduring themes of the biblical narrative is the release from bondage to freedom.

Not only the release from captivity, but the ongoing story of the desert experience; to not only take the people out of Egypt – but to take Egypt out of the people.

The destination is the Promised Land, and the desert is the place of preparation.

Even after entering the Promised Land, the battle still rages between the flesh and the Spirit; and between freedom and bondage.

Part of the battle plan is self-examination. We lift Jesus up as the children of Israel lifted the serpent in the wilderness. By lifting Him up in the process of examining our lives, we expose the effect of the world and the culture has made on our walk.

We expose the bite of the serpent (the impact worldly values have had on our lives).

We are called to be followers of Jesus and to die to self. The covenants are a continuous process of accomplishing this responsibility.

As we are obedient, the Holy Spirit will reveal areas of our lives that need repentance and grace.

Dallas Willard told us we don't need to try harder, but we need to train. Sabbath Economics is part of the training process.

Our journey from bondage to freedom is a constant struggle against addiction and idols.

We need to be very diligent to the formation of unseen addictions and idol formation. (see Isaiah 2:8, Psalm 135:16, 2 John 5:21)

Addictions and idols are bad, but the worst thing they enslave is a person's will and desire. They divert and suppress the energy of desire to love and to be loved by God. We become attached to this in a process that enslaves desire and creates the state of addiction.

I am designed to secure God's love and allow that love to flow to other people. Love is the source and to love is the goal.

Freedom in the truest sense is the removal of all things in myself that impede the flow of that love.

Through grace, the dynamic life of God in me gives the desire and the power to remove my addictions and idols. I can be a conduit for God's love. My total orientation to the world is by the desire to let love flow uncontested and unimpeded.

> Search me, O God, and know my heart!
> Try me and know my thoughts!
> Psalm 135:23

Sabbath is a way to allow the Lord to search my heart.

Bill Robertson
William F. Robertson & Associates

My Story

◆ ◆ ◆

This little book is my attempt to show ways that culture has influenced us and how practically we can go in a different direction. Specifically, I have drawn heavily on Ched Myers' teaching of Sabbath Economics based upon the story of the manna in Exodus and selected teachings of Jesus, specifically *the lilies of the field.* Sabbath Economics stresses that our God is a God of "enough." He is providing everything we need.

To make the teaching easier to digest, Ched developed seven covenants as follows:

- ***Surplus Capital*** – addresses how we invest our surplus;
- ***Negative Capital*** – details the dangers of debt;
- ***Giving*** – our God is a generous God and he wants us to share in that joy;
- ***God's Creation*** – everything is connected through Jesus (Colossians 1:16) and we should treat the earth as such;
- ***Consumption*** – how we spend money is a direct reflection of our faith;
- ***Solidarity*** – entails deliberately spending time with those less fortunate whom God has shown a preferential option;
- ***Work and Sabbath*** – for me, the hardest of the covenants. Our work, and observation of the Sabbath, is a direct reflection of our trust.

These covenants are easy to include in your life and can be transformational.

The covenant that really stood out to me, and still does, is that of **solidarity**: intentionally spending time with those of a different economic class. I failed in my attempts to volunteer in several prison ministries and food closets. Even though the efforts were not successful, I noticed the interconnectedness of the other covenants.

That, I think, is the "secret" of Sabbath Economics: seeing that connectedness. Working on one discipline or covenant at a time can lead to pride. I can give generously while struggling greatly with the rest of my walk. I can work to retire my debt (i.e. negative capital), but in the end such activities can be inwardly focused.

By looking at one covenant and its relation to others, I felt like I began to see the heart or mind of God not visible to me before. I began to see so many things that I had taken for granted or were not reality. The emphasis on **solidarity** influenced my **giving** to be targeted towards helping the poor. I attempted to keep savings at banks that operate in lower income neighborhoods (**surplus capital**). In **God's creation**, the environment began to take on more importance as I realized Jesus' existence in everything. Though I admit that I am very slow to change in the area of **work and Sabbath**, I am trying more and more to realize that it is God, not me, that provides. And finally, my **consumption** habits are changing as I think how much more precious the money would be in the hands of those less fortunate.

Preparatory work did influence the impact of Sabbath Economics. I have been involved in stewardship for many years. In addition to being involved with various biblical counselors, Mike Little of the Faith and Money Network took me through the *money autobiography* process. I came to Sabbath Economics with some idea of my ingrained habits and addictions.

Over the last few years, my journey has radically changed. No longer are my finances just a part of my faith. I am more and more beginning to understand, as Richard Rohr says, "It all belongs." I am beginning to see how I have compartmentalized my faith. I hope that I am becoming more whole. My new journey is sometimes painful, but there is no place I would rather be.

These covenants or disciplines, are biblical, widely accepted, and can only strengthen your walk. In and of themselves, they do not require a lot of physical effort. As the term covenant implies, commitment is important. Speaking only for myself, I do not know my final destination. I assume many twists and turns will continue along the way. I just know that it is important to be moving, and our program performs that function.

The word "repent" is often used in Christianity with the meaning "to turn from sin and dedicate oneself to the amendment of one's life." I like another definition of the word, namely, **"to change one's mind."**[1] I feel that is what the covenants of Sabbath Economics are doing in my life-changing my mind, giving me a different outlook, causing me to go in a different direction. A new path or direction does not require much additional effort. What is required is direction. Sabbath Economics more aligns actions with values reducing anxiety.

G. Richard Truitt, Jr.

Introduction

Overwhelming!

The problems we face are overwhelming:

- A loss of values, integrity, an awe of God.
- Poverty, starvation, people killing people.
- Job security is increasingly uncertain.
- Bills have to be paid.
- Expenses keep rising.
- Global economic slowdown.
- Looming environmental catastrophes.

All the while, you are trying to be a good parent, a good spouse, a good son or daughter. And above everything else, you are called to be a Christian.

We All Wonder, "Will I Have Enough?"

Jesus said, "My yoke is easy, and my burden is light." (Matthew 11:30). Did He mean that life was supposed to be easy? Or did He mean that if you arrange your life according to Him, the 'overwhelm' would decrease?

We are an anxious people. We are like the Israelites, wandering in the wilderness and hoping for Egypt (Exodus 16:2–3); taking comfort in the familiar even if the familiar is not comfortable.

We feel in our bones that something is wrong. We feel, hope – *maybe even know* – that there is something better. We look to a promised land. The world and its power structure are changing.

As widely reported, for the first time in our history, Americans expect their children to experience a more turbulent society and lifestyle than themselves[2]. It seems as if a cold wind is beginning to blow. (We spoke about some of this in our webinar *The Fourth Turning*.)

We are anxious because of many reasons. Much of our anxiety is because we live "in the tension," in between acting from selfish interests and acting as we think we should. This tension causes guilt in addition to anxiety. We look to God for a certainty that we will never find this side of heaven. Anxiety will always be with us, but then how shall we live?

Peter Rollins, a northern Irish theologian and writer, tells the following story of his "cousin" Seamus.

> There was once a very rich Texan who started to look into his ancestral roots. After a little research, he discovered that his Great Grandfather left Ireland to settle in America and that there was a relative of his called Seamus, who still had a small farm in Galway.
>
> The next day he flew out to visit Seamus and reconnect with his roots. When he finally found the farm, he knocked on the door and introduced himself.
>
> "Would you like to see the property?" said Seamus to his guest. "Why, yes." So, Seamus took the large Texan round to the back of the little house and pointed at a tree that stood about fifty feet away.
>
> "See that tree?" he said. "That marks the northern boundary of my land." Then he pointed at a rusty old tractor in the distance. "That there marks the western border. And that," he said, pointing to a broken fence, "marks the eastern border."
>
> "Well," said the Texan with a patronizing smile, "back home, if I got into my car and drove all day north, I still wouldn't reach the border of my land. Indeed, if I drove all day east or west, I wouldn't get to the border of my property."
>
> "Yeah," said Seamus while nodding, "I know how you feel. I used to have a car like that."[3]

Seamus has a grasp on a true reality which the Texan has not yet found. Seamus has made friends with the anxiety and no longer needs material possessions to fill what Pascal called a God shaped hole. This "grasp" can be expressed by the Greek word **telos**, usually defined as "end," "purpose," or "goal."[4] Aristotle used the term as one of his four causations of change. In the fifth century, Augustine used the term to describe the apparent purpose of the universe in his "proof" of God.[5] It is often said, as a culture, we lack telos. Nothing of lasting value undergirds our actions. How much do we structure our life along Tommy Airey's definition of a Christian telos: *participate with God in the healing and redemption of the world?*[6]

Could this new telos be what Jesus Christ meant by "lose your life"? We are so much a part of the materialistic culture we live in, that like the Texan, we need to die to that materialistic myth to find peace and rest. Our capitalistic society is built around scarcity. Resources are finite and we can never have enough. The God of abundance (as we shall see) promises more, but with persecutions[7]. To trust in Him, to have "faith," requires community, a lifetime, and most importantly, Him.

Sabbath Economics is a *means* (described further below) to search out this telos, a framework to live more like the *master of the God-designed life* (as Eugene Peterson translates in 1 Corinthians 1:8). Rooted in the manna story of Exodus 16 and the birds of the air passage from Matthew 6, The Sabbath was one of the practices instituted by God to limit self to let God's love flow through us to others. He is enough. Sabbath Economics is a way to pay attention to what is important to God and refocus our priorities to their proper place. By addressing personal financial issues, progress is – in a sense – measurable and hard to fake to others and ourselves.

Dr. Walter Brueggeman, Old Testament scholar and theologian, wrote "For those who are living in anxiety and fear, most especially fear of scarcity, have no time or energy for the common good."[8]

What is this "common good?" I think it corresponds to our concept of telos. Not only do we need to define this common good/telos for ourselves, but; as Brueggeman states, we need to address our anxiety and fear which block our pursuit. Telos is possibly what life is all about. This book does not propose to tackle such a weighty topic in total, but it does explore one of the methods with this end in mind – Sabbath Economics.

I mentioned Pascal's God shaped hole that we attempt to fill with material possessions. This hole (or "lack" to use Peter Rollins' term) is painful. We attempt to control our surroundings because of fear of this pain. And our inability to control our situation results in anger or anxiety thus blocking our desire, or using all our energy, to pursue our telos.[9]

How do we reduce anxiety and fear so the common good within us can come forth? The late Dallas Willard's concept of ***VIM*** draws on the idea of telos, narrows it down, and makes it personable and actionable.[10]

VIM is an acronym composed of the following:

> ***Vision*** – where you are trying to go;
> ***Intention*** – what you believe that gives you the drive to pursue the vision;
> ***Means*** – the actual tasks that you will use, motivated by the intention, to reach (but also find) the vision.

I believe *vision* coupled with *intention* can be thought of as telos. And as mentioned, the *means* (which Sabbath Economics is just but one of many) is how you walk out your telos.

Vision

A vision is different for every individual, is hard to nail down, and changes over time. But the vision is an important, if not the most important, aspect to your life. *Where there is no vision, the people perish....*[11]

If you are having trouble with the vision concept, consider theologian Frederick Buechner's quote, "The place God calls you to is the place where your deep gladness and the world's deep hunger meet."[12]

Intention

I cannot explain *intention*, but it is perhaps most important of the three. I think it must be God-given. A statement by Frank Schaeffer, the son of the famous evangelist Francis Schaeffer helped me:

> Well, the reason I didn't leave faith altogether is one that I'll never know because I don't know where my conditioning as a person of faith begins and where my choices begin and where they end. All I can tell you is that if I wanted to become an atheist, the first thing I would do is pray to God to help me and that probably tells you that I'm stuck. And I'm stuck because faith is just part of my life. I don't know whether it's because faith is real or whether it's because that's the way I was brought up. But a day that doesn't begin with prayer for me feels empty, even when I'm questioning the existence of God. And that's just who I am. And so, for me, I had to wash up in some sort of a faith community or feel that a limb was missing.[13]

Schaeffer could not explain why he kept trying to relate to God, just that he did.

The big question is always, "Why do we do what we do?" Like *vision*, *intention* is hard to nail down. Eugene Peterson's translation of Colossians 1:5 is, "The lines of purpose in your lives never grow slack, tightly tied as they are to your future in heaven, kept taut by hope." These *lines of purpose* that are *tightly tied in heaven* cannot be explained in human terms.

Hildegard, a 12th-century saint, spoke often of *viriditas*, the greening of things.[14] As plants have a readiness to receive the sun, there is an inherent readiness within us to respond to the "divine

Presence." Another 12th-century saint, Bernard of Clairvaux, taught that humanity was created with a desire to be in motion towards a goal or telos. "God's presence, God's desire, God's love, evokes our desire."[15]

Maybe *intentionality* is our desire for fullness. Maybe *intentionality* is a desire to be "right" or favored by God. All I know is something, *some lines of purpose*, draws me to what I think of as "spiritual" work.

The different types of "*means*" exceed the human imagination. This book is an exploration of the covenants or *means* of Sabbath Economics. As illustrated below, *vision*, *intention*, and *means* all inform each other in a continuous creative work.

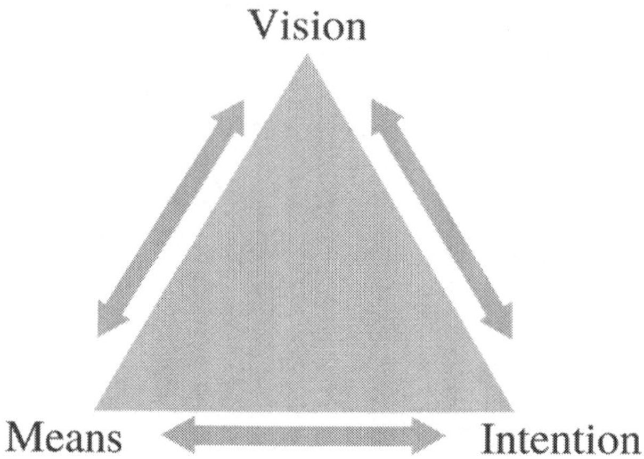

Pop singer Rachel Platten's song "Stand by You" contains the following lyrics:[16]

> Oh, truth – I guess truth is what you believe in
> And faith – I think faith is having a reason.

Truth can correspond to **vision**; faith to **intention**. The song also contains:

Even if we can't find heaven,
I'll walk through hell with you.

We will probably always have anxiety, but the comfort comes from knowing you do not have to go through this alone. Or as beautifully put by John Caputo, "The voice that consoles, the hand that gently touches, the vow to be with you through this long night, to stay by your side, the promise, absolute and unconditional, to be there when you awake...."[17] For me, that is the essence of the Gospel.

The model (a collection of disciplines or "*means*") described in this book is designed to create space for a manageable change in your financial life more towards your telos. To figure out what one's growing edge is and to work *that*. Each person and household is where it is, and can only begin *there*. The only relevant question is: "What are the *next* steps I/we can and will take to journey deeper into a relationship with God here and now, in the context in which I live and work (telos)?" No step is considered too small and no step too large.

I can only speak for myself, but I know if a problem is overwhelming or too daunting, I tend to do nothing. Looking only at those things I can control, and taking baby steps to affect those things, seems like a doable method. Small choices made deliberately and with conviction seem to be the most lasting.

Contrary to the society we live in, "success" in each endeavor is not the goal. Focusing on one task can result in pride of personal accomplishment instead of fulfilling telos. University of Texas marketing professor Raj Raghunathan suggests that a "dispassionate pursuit of passion" is necessary for happiness.[18] Or as Thomas Merton said in a February 21, 1966 letter to a friend:

> Do not depend on the hope of results. While you are doing this sort of work you have taken on, essentially an apostolic work, you may have to face the fact that your work will be apparently worthless and achieve no results at all, if not perhaps results opposite to what you expect.[19]

The journey is much more important than the destination. Do not attempt to change the world to fit your perception of God's will, but live more of the "true you" with the knowledge that God resides within (Colossians 1:27, 1 Corinthians 3:16). This model could be wrong (and just ask my wife, I have been wrong before), but, in the spirit of Pascal's Wager (the stakes are so high to alone justify belief), can you afford or even want to continue living your life in your present direction?

It is Possible to Live Unknowingly in Bondage

Some have said that the hypocrisy of the Pharisees of which Jesus spoke in Matthew 16:6 is sometimes translated as "mismatch." Anxiety arises because we are not acting, i.e. there is a mismatch, between our actions (sometimes caused by unknown bondage) and our hearts. We lack integrity, i.e. wholeness.

The suggested small steps (see: *A Sample First Step* under *Surplus* chapter), are only worthwhile if God is in the work (1 Corinthians 3:11–15). As Jan Johnson suggests in her article on the Twelve Step model of Alcoholics Anonymous, we should "use spiritual disciplines as experiments, not rules."[20] The teaching of Sabbath Economics contains within it model practices which I treat as spiritual disciplines. These disciplines are only worth doing with God, through God, and with the power of God.

I know of no way of determining the appropriate discipline except to try it, as it is impossible to know with certainty, that one is doing the "right" thing. Even the martyrs that were burned at the stake, it is my understanding, were not completely sure they were following God's will. Yet, without an attraction towards the means, *intentionality* will not be strong enough to carry you forward. Killian Noe, founder of Recovery Café, relates how you must be doing something you love to be successful.[21] Or as referenced by 19th century pastor Thomas Chalmers, "*the expulsive power of a new affection.*"[22]

Sabbath Economics involves covenants, i.e. movement and doing. In my experience, the "doing" of the covenant enables you to experience the heart and mind of God as you begin to see the relationships between the remaining covenants. As Richard Rohr said, "We do not think ourselves into a new way of living, but we live ourselves into a new way of thinking."[23]

Anxiety underlies our efforts to make perceptions fit reality. Nassim Taleb, in his book *Antifragile*, tells the tale of Procrustes from Greek mythology.[24] Procrustes when inviting guests into his home, rather than adjust or find a good fitting bed, would strangely either stretch or amputate parts of his guest's legs to make them fit. Taleb likens Procrustes to the way we sometimes view the world. We contort our life, our investment systems, etc., to fit tidy theories.

Richard Rohr again writes, "There are commonly two kinds of human beings: there are people who want certitude and there are people who want understanding...."[25] Anxiously we search for certitude where we are promised none. Becoming comfortable with an uncertain reality, I think, is the goal of faith.

- We need to remain flexible in our service, but the desire for flexibility should not limit our activities;
- We know our view of the world is tainted (Matthew 7:3) and we should be alert as the Spirit clarifies our view; and
- Structuring your life per your values, instead of the world's, involves risk-but that risk can be a source of strength as opposed to weakness.

Need for Self-Evaluation

A scene from *The Horse and the Boy*, the fifth book in CS Lewis's beloved series, *The Chronicles of Narnia*, has always stuck with me. The horse and his boy (remember the animals in Narnia are personified and can talk) are racing to warn of a pending invasion.

The horse is convinced he is running as fast and hard as he can. A lion (which we later discover to be Aslan, a representation of Jesus Christ) chases the horse causing the horse to run even faster.

Sometimes our mind convinces us that we are doing the best we can. Sometimes God shows us that more is possible.

Much of Sabbath Economics involves self-evaluation. Though long ago it was said "The unexamined life is not worth living,"[26] the pursuit of meaning in one's life can become an idol. As we shall see, the human heart can become addicted or attached to just about anything. A balance seems most important.

Consider the words found in Ecclesiastes,

> Everyone also to whom God has given wealth and possessions and power to enjoy them, and to accept his lot and rejoice in his toil — this is the gift of God. For he will not much remember the days of his life because God keeps him occupied with joy in his heart. ~ Ecclesiastes 5:19–20

Dr. David G Brenner wrote the following, "There really is nothing more important than finding God and myself — but we will only do so when we realize that truly this is but a single task!"[27]

The Red Pill or the Blue Pill?

> You take the blue pill, the story ends. You wake up in your bed and believe whatever you want to believe. You take the red pill, you stay in Wonderland, and I show you how deep the rabbit hole goes. ~ Morpheus, to Neo in the movie *The Matrix*[28]

I guess there is something to be said about remaining "fat, dumb, and happy." Pursuing the effort, which is often painful, in search of telos seems like the only way to live a life of flourishing.

> I didn't say it would be easy, Neo. I just said it would be the truth.[29] ~ Morpheus

Lessons from a Prophet

I think an analogy from an account found in Ezekiel can help demonstrate this idea. Barry Taylor, of Homebrewed Christianity, recounts a vision, about stages of spiritual growth as defined by Scott Peck (of *The Road Less Traveled* fame), found in Ezekiel 47: 3–6.[30] In the vision, Ezekiel is taken through the desert to the temple. Water flows from each side of the Temple bringing life to the New World.

- First Ezekiel is guided out 1,000 cubits to where the water is ankle-deep. This represents the chaos, an uncontrolled reorganization, when one first begins to walk with God.
- Ezekiel is guided out another thousand cubits where the water is knee-deep. Per the model, this is as deep is most churchgoers go. They experience some of God, but they are in complete control, more of their body is out of the water than in.
- Out another thousand cubits, the water is waist deep. Anxiety is ever-present because of the pushing of the water.

According to Peck, people in the third stage of spiritual growth have the principles of goodness "engraved on their hearts." Thus, they no longer need the forms of society or a church to keep their behavior in check. They are self-governing.

Because they no longer need the services offered by a church, they begin to feel free to question the value of religion in their lives. They may at this point choose to reject religious belief.

Even though they may describe themselves as atheist or agnostic, people in Stage III are actually more spiritually developed than most of those content to remain in Stage II. They are often deeply committed to social causes. They are active seekers of truth.[31]

- Then, at another thousand cubits, the waters become a river "a river that I could not pass through, for the water had risen. It was deep enough to swim in, river that could not be passed through...." This is the territory of the mystics, the territory I think Richard Rohr refers to in his book *Breathing Underwater* (I have included the book's underlying poem in Appendix C). A territory of mystery, surrender to God, a place where you know where you are supposed to be. Unfortunately, this territory is beyond the author's experience and thus this book.

- Lastly, Ezekiel is turned back to shore where the bank has changed from barren desert to forest. I think the time in the water is where one obtains the God-given vision and God-given intentionality, the telos. But you must return to the shore to do your good work, i.e. the means. In this way, the three components of *VIM* inform each other. The vision and intentionality (telos) point to the appropriate means (the greening of the shore), the means point to the telos (where to enter the water).

Paraphrasing the Brueggeman quote, *those living in anxiety and fear have no energy for telos*. The hope of this book is to reduce anxiety and the fear of scarcity by suggesting a way of looking at and acting in the world. These suggestions are *means* found in the form of stewardship called Sabbath Economics as developed by Ched Myers. But these *means* are as of "wood, hay, straw" (I Corinthians 3:12) unless a more complete way to live your life, a *vision* and *intentionality*, a **telos**, develops.

1

Stewardship and Sabbath Economics

◆ ◆ ◆

We are called to stewardship.

Webster's defines stewardship as follows: *the activity or job of protecting and being responsible for something.*[32] This definition is different than the way the word is commonly used in our churches, i.e. for a capital campaign. The concept of biblical stewardship is normally based upon Psalm 24:1, "*The earth is the Lord's and the fullness thereof, the world and those who dwell therein....*" Frankly, I'm not sure what to do with that verse. I do not feel that it permeates my life very much.

From my volunteer stewardship work, I was very familiar with the following verse:

> Moreover, it is required of stewards that they be found faithful.
> ~ 1 Corinthians 4:2

Until I read John C. Haughey's book, *Virtue and Affluence*, I assumed that the word *stewards* pertained to the management of physical resources. However, consider the previous verse which specifies the object of the stewardship as follows:

> This is how one should regard us, as servants of Christ and stewards of the mysteries of God. ~ 1 Corinthians 4:1

Haughey states, and I think correctly, that we are **first** to steward the mysteries of God and then we can begin to know how to properly steward the physical resources He has given us. That first-order stewardship is only done with prayer and community, without which stewardship becomes only about calculation ("calculus of the Pharisees"). Because sin is what separates us from the mysteries of God, we need to "...lay aside every weight, and sin which clings so closely, and let us run with endurance the race that is set before us." ~ Hebrews 12:1

Stewardship and Discipleship

Haughey further states, "If stewardship does not come from discipleship, then stewardship turns into a batch of 'oughts.'"[33] Ched Meyer's Sabbath Economics develops this discipleship (or means), in which we can discover a framework to uncover hidden sins and contemplate more of these *mysteries of God*. Like spiritual disciplines, the doing of the covenants are not helpful in and of themselves. However, these activities instruct the body (i.e. "get you out of your head") and create space to better contemplate *the mysteries*. This is not as complex as it sounds.

Stewardship is a part of discipleship. Everyone's discipleship or *means*, like their *vision*, is unique. As "God leads each one along different paths."[34] No one, except God Himself, can tell you how to handle your money. As Paul indicates in 1 Corinthians 4 we are to guide, not instruct, each other to help seek these mysteries in our hearts. Again, we need prayer and we need community. As anxiety appears always present in our lives, especially when we are *going in a different direction*, the support of others is critical.

Theologian Richard Lowery defines Sabbath Economics as follows:

> ...a way of living in the world that starts from the assumption that it's possible for everyone to have enough to thrive. Scarcity and poverty are not 'the will of God.' They are failures of human imagination, departures from the dream God has for the world. Sabbath Economics assumes that everyone can have enough. It is

grounded in a conscious choice to place limits on our own work and consumption.[35]

Contrast the foregoing with the two main axioms of classical economics:

- The assumed condition of scarcity
- Unlimited individual appetite[36]

God's ways, living in His kingdom, entails continued reorienting to true reality.

Stewardship and Abundance

Yes, the Bible tells us God is a God of abundance. Though He placed us on this earth with sufficient resources, we must be realistic and understand those resources are also limited.

Daniel Bell writes, "Proclaiming God's abundance does not deny the reality of scarcity. What it does is locate the origin of scarcity where it belongs, namely, in sin."[37] Yet in common with most, I struggle greatly with this mindset. Researchers have shown an abundance mindset results in more happiness.[38] Though the scarcity mindset is needed at times, this mindset (which is my default) promotes anxiety. As discussed further in Chapter 2, the abundance mindset is more characteristic of His kingdom, the scarcity mindset characterizes our earthly kingdom.

Sabbath Economics is largely grounded in the story of the Israelites in the wilderness. After God heard the Israelites grumble about hunger in the wilderness, he produced the bread-like substance *manna* to feed the Israelites. He gave specific instructions for the gathering of the substance. Each was to gather enough only for that day, with there being "no lack." The exception to the limited gathering was for the sixth day where each was to gather enough for that day *and* the Sabbath. The Sabbath was to be a day of rest.

> And when the dew had gone up, there was on the face of the wilderness a fine, flake-like thing, fine as frost on the ground. When the people of Israel saw it, they said to one another, "What is it?" For they did not know what it was. And Moses said to them, "It is the bread that the Lord has given you to eat. This is what the Lord has commanded: 'Gather of it, each one of you, as much as he can eat. You shall each take an omer, according to the number of the persons that each of you has in his tent.'" And the people of Israel did so. They gathered, some more, some less. But when they measured it with an omer, whoever gathered much had nothing left over, and whoever gathered little had no lack. Each of them gathered as much as he could eat. ~ Exodus 16:14–18

God responded to the Israelites' scarcity mindset out of his abundance.

The Sabbath rest is further outlined in Leviticus 25. The Israelites are instructed to allow the land to rest every seven years, with all debts canceled. In addition, in the 50th year of Jubilee, land was to be returned to the original owners. With a philosophy of scarcity, idleness or not working can be a great source of anxiety. The Sabbath rest directly confronts that mindset. The Sabbath year prevented permanent poverty or a permanent underclass. Though it is not clear that the Israelites ever practiced the Sabbath year or Jubilee, Jesus' first sermon (found in Luke 4) is from Isaiah 61 declaring the year of Jubilee. Thus, Jesus reiterated the tradition of Jubilee.

> The Spirit of the Lord is upon me, because he has anointed me to proclaim good news to the poor. He has sent me to proclaim liberty to the captives and recovering of sight to the blind, to set at liberty those who are oppressed, to proclaim the year of the Lord's favor. ~ Luke 4:18–19

Consider the following:

> Therefore, I tell you, do not be anxious about your life, what you will eat or what you will drink, nor about your body, what you will

> put on. Is not life more than food, and the body more than clothing? Look at the birds of the air: they neither sow nor reap nor gather into barns, and yet your heavenly Father feeds them. Are you not of more value than they? And which of you by being anxious can add a single hour to his span of life? And why are you anxious about clothing? Consider the lilies of the field, how they grow: they neither toil nor spin, yet I tell you, even Solomon in all his glory was not arrayed like one of these. But if God so clothes the grass of the field, which today is alive and tomorrow is thrown into the oven, will he not much more clothe you, O you of little faith? Therefore, do not be anxious, saying, 'What shall we eat?' or 'What shall we drink?' or 'What shall we wear?' For the Gentiles seek after all these things, and your heavenly Father knows that you need them all. But seek first the kingdom of God and his righteousness, and all these things will be added to you. Therefore, do not be anxious about tomorrow, for tomorrow will be anxious for itself. Sufficient for the day is its own trouble. ~ Matthew 6:25–34

The spirit of Sabbath Economics is one of dependence upon God, living in His ways, and caring for His people and creation. In our materialistic culture, the competition for our desires is intense. Our flesh cries out for security – security in things that can be seen. We attempt to control our futures with our plans. We fool ourselves, and I am afraid God laughs at us. The variables that we know, in conjunction more so with the mind of God that we do not know, make any certainty with respect to the future an illusion. Our addiction to security, a disordered love, can only be called a sin.

Jesus instructed us to "seek first the kingdom of God." Apparently, this is at least partially, if not mostly, what it means to be a disciple. How do we go about that? What does the "kingdom of God" mean? Consider the concept of the *two kingdoms*.

- John Calvin distinguished "the spiritual kingdom of Christ" from "the civil kingdom."
- Augustine wrote of the "city of God" and "earthly city."

- Wendell Berry uses the terms “the great economy” and “the little economy.”

We like the terms “Heavenly Kingdom” and “earthly kingdom.” Even the language of these two kingdoms is similar. For example:

> And my God will supply every need of yours according to his riches in glory in Christ Jesus. ~ Philippians 4:19

> But whatever gain I had, I counted as loss for the sake of Christ. ~ Philippians 3:7

> So is the one who lays up treasure for himself and is not rich toward God. ~ Luke 12:21

> The kingdom of heaven is like treasure hidden in the field, which a man found and covered up. Then in his joy he goes and sells all he has and buys that field. Again, the kingdom of heaven is like a merchant in search of fine pearls, who, on finding one pearl of great value, went and sold all that he had and bought it. ~ Matthew 13:44–46

> ...that though he was rich, yet for your sake he became poor, so that you by his poverty might become rich. ~ II Corinthians 8:9

> ...and raised us up with him and seated us with him in the heavenly places in Christ Jesus, so that in the coming ages he may show the immeasurable riches of his grace in kindness towards us in Christ Jesus. ~ Ephesians 2:6–7

Though the Heavenly Kingdom is obviously greater than the earthly kingdom, the rules for both are important and should be respected.

2

Living a Wonderful Life within Two Kingdoms

◆ ◆ ◆

... stuff of earth competes for the allegiance. ~ Rich Mullins

A perennial Christmas time favorite is the movie, *It's a Wonderful Life*. The movie is the story of George Bailey, played by James Stewart, who runs Bailey Brothers Building and Loan Association. The town's other financial institution is run by Henry F. Potter. Whereas the Building and Loan concentrates on mortgages to blue-collar working people, Potter values profits. And as shown by Clarence, George Bailey's guardian angel, a future with Potter as the town's main businessman is not attractive.

I believe Frank Capra's protagonists in the movie exemplify two ways of life – or life in two different "kingdoms." Potter lives entirely within the earthly kingdom. Except for hiding the Building and Loan's lost deposit, we do not see Potter actually breaking the law. And Bailey is hardly selfless. He longs for a life of world travel and accomplishments. Both, but especially Potter, are aware of the rules of the earthly kingdom.

Bailey values people more than profits. His business practices move him more to this heavenly kingdom. Through George Bailey's experiences, we are shown what can happen when the rules of both kingdoms, one heavenly and one earthly, are not respected.

Unfortunately, in real life, the heavenly kingdom, God's kingdom, is all too often forgotten or ignored.

As Dr. Richard Swenson, M.D. in his book *Contentment* says, "Love is the currency of this kingdom. The currency of the earthly kingdom is money. We need both, but their differences must be respected. We are commanded to seek the Kingdom of God *first*, but not exclusively."[39]

John Haughey in his book *The Holy Use of Money* speaks of the union of these two kingdoms. We need both as they keep us from becoming too worldly and too world-escaping. Difficult yes, but attempting to operate in the Heavenly kingdom while living in this earthly kingdom, says Haughey, is a way to truly appreciate Christ. This tension, living in God's abundance while on this planet of limited resources, is a source of anxiety. The tension will not go away this side of heaven, but we can learn how to live in these two kingdoms well.

> In so many areas of life, you need to be a long-term optimist but a short-term realist.[40] ~ Chelsey "Sully" Sullenberger, the pilot who safely landed US Airways flight 1549 in the Hudson River, saving all aboard

Where You Really Live

The Puritans, as religious as they were, had a difficult time applying values from the heavenly kingdom to everyday life.[41] The same difficulty may apply to us today, more than we realize.

Stanley Hauerwas, one of America's most quoted theologians, suggests we look to the role of an ambassador as an example for our lives in this world. In other words, the laws of our home country rule, but we also need to know local customs and laws.[42] Or as Dwight Edwards puts it, "The believer is called to live with his feet planted in this world while his heart is held captive by the next."[43]

Our deep longing for purpose and substance and meaning has been met in Christ. Yet, how often do believers in Jesus still live out of a restlessness produced by anxiety, rather than living in that rest produced by knowing (and believing) that it is finished?

Our age, it seems, is an age of anxiety. We are an anxious people. Those who are not worried about retirement, sending kids to college, the economy, declining social values, terrorists etc., are often viewed by the rest as those who are just not paying attention! (Or as Anne Lamott quipped, "It is fine if you believe that there is some cute bumper sticker silver lining, but for the love of God, PLEASE keep it to yourself. It will just tense us all up."[44])

The future seems so uncertain. And as Julie Beck wrote in *The Atlantic*, "uncertainty seems to be a necessary condition for anxiety of any kind."[45]

Society is anxious because of:

- Greed: We want more
- Entitlement: We think we are due ("To be born in America is to be given a Ph.D. in entitlement."[46])
- Envy: We want what others have.[47]

Carl Richards, a financial planner in Park City, Utah, and director of investor education at the BAM Alliance, offers this unusual formula: Uncertainty = Reality.[48] Perhaps this is where you are currently living?

Mike Wilkerson in his book *Redemption: Freed by Jesus from the Idols We Worship and the Wounds We Carry* states, "Anxiety is a shade of fear, which is the flipside of desire. You want something, and you're afraid you won't get it. Or you have something you're afraid to lose. Either way, you're on edge, agitated, discontent... ."[49] And "fear," writes author Max Lucado, "at its center, is a perceived loss of control."[50] Stanley Hauerwas, again wrote, "Our nation, allegedly the strongest in the world, runs on fear. The American people are frightened to death."[51] And, as well-known psychologist and teacher Dr. Larry Crabb puts it, "[Anxiety is] living for a purpose that you have no guarantee is going to be realized. You're demanding a particular goal for your own well-being but you know way down deep that God isn't agreeing with that goal as something that he guarantees."[52] Crabb further suggests, "Think of anxiety as the red light flashing on your dashboard."[53]

Sabbath Economics addresses anxiety by learning more the mind of God and aligning yourself with His purposes. He created you (Genesis 2:7), he created you with a purpose (Ephesians 1:11), and much of the source of anxiety is us trying to live life as we see fit, on our terms.

John Haughey points out that Jesus's ministry was a way of life, "...that was never without material needs and the necessity to procure them. He would've been tempted to anxiety all his life. He calls his followers to deal with it as he did." Haughey concludes that, "Material and financial hopes that are not in alignment with one's religious faith and hope will begin to afflict persons with anxiety...."[54]

We may numb our sensitivities to this anxiety with drugs or entertainment diversions, with the attendant detriments to our physical health.[55] We may also handle this anxiety through what Oswald Chambers describes as "sentimentality" – saying one thing but doing another – which can result in many troubles, including the idolatry discussed below:

> Sentimentality has to be ignored. Jesus Christ said – "You call me Master and Lord, but you don't what I say." That is the gist of the failure of Christianity; it has been tried and abandoned because it is been found difficult, but has never failed when it has been tried and gone on with honourably.[56]

Sentimentality has been called the greatest enemy to American Christianity.[57]

These anxieties, fears, etc., cause pain. As humans, we strive to reduce the pain driving addiction and attachment. Even if one conceptually knows the only true source of life in the universe is God, our subconscious works overtime in trying to find an easier way.

Gerald G. May wrote the definitive book on this subject entitled *Addiction and Grace*. His take on the matter is this, "I am not being flippant when I say that all of us suffer from addiction."[58] And May further writes, "No matter how religious we may think we are, our addictions are always capable of usurping our concern for God."[59]

The object of our addictions and attachments is usually an idol, a false idol. For example, the Israelites in the Exodus turned from Moses to the golden calf in a vain attempt to gain some certainty with the absence of Moses (Exodus 32). Instead of embracing our emotions, we attempt to alleviate the pain caused by anxiety, our misplaced hopes and failure to live up to our words, with idols.

As mentioned, the good thing about spiritual matters from a financial standpoint is that finances are very hard to fake. It is easy to say, "I love my neighbor" because it is difficult to prove. However, because one's giving is very measurable, not being as generous as claimed can easily give rise to an idol, and associated addiction, of personal comfort.

Stuff on Earth

The prohibition against idolatry is the first of the 10 Commandments, "You shall have no other gods before me." (Exodus 20:3). The evil of idolatry, as Norman Wirzba in his book *From Nature to Creation* states, is one of humanity's worst sins. "We confuse something given by God as a means of life with its being the source and fulfillment of life. False worship is so dangerous because it witnesses to human attention and energy being directed in ways that are bound to lead to mutual harm."[60] He quotes Athanasius, "The prime cause, therefore, of idolatry is evil.[61] "Just as Augustine taught that "idolatry was the root of all sin."[62]

Evil can be thought of originating in three places, the body being one of those places. We are all very familiar with sin that originates within us. We are exhorted to try harder and to refrain from certain activities to be more "holy."

But evil also is evidenced in systemic sin originating outside the body. Since these are, by their very nature commended by society, they are very hard to see. For instance, lust is looked down upon us on an individual basis, but is acceptable in our capitalist system for use in marketing. Killing is against the law, but if sanctioned by the society for war, it is "good."

Even harder to see are the evil and resulting idols that are the products of our consumer capitalistic society such as "progress" or "materialism." These idols will continue to result in sin at the individual level unless addressed. One Catholic priest reports that he has never heard a confession relating to the 10th commandment!

> You shall not covet your neighbor's house; you shall not covet your neighbor's wife, or his male servant, or his female servant, or his ox, or his donkey, or anything that is your neighbor's. ~ Exodus 20:17

Such a confession would be against capitalism and would be unthinkable. Much of this evil arises out of the obvious conflict. As Frederick Bastiat stated in his treatise, *Economic Sophisms*, "The world's current economic system creates a conflict between the buyer and the seller. The buyer obviously wants things abundant and cheap, whereas the seller wants products to be scarce and expensive."[63]

The implications of living in this conflict, of the pain caused by the lack of control, are enormous. The stuff of earth has, for too long, been winning the war for our affections.

◆ ◆ ◆

We must rapidly begin the shift from a 'thing-oriented' society to a 'person-oriented' society. When machines and computers, profit motives and property rights are considered more important than people, the giant triplets of racism, materialism, and militarism are incapable of being conquered. ~ Martin Luther King, Jr. [64]

3

The Economics of Idol Addiction

◆ ◆ ◆

By locating the challenges for Christian discipleship in arcane cults or sexual temptations or the "secularizing" forces of the Supreme Court, evangelism tends to miss the fact that the great tempter of our age is Walmart.
~ James K.A. Smith, forward to The Economy of Desire[65]

Addiction has been defined as "needing more and more of what is not working." In that sense, we are indeed an addictive society because we have not found a solid source and ground for our dignity. We always look for it outside of ourselves, and thus it is intrinsically based on a model of scarcity, where the source can be taken away, where "I" am not enough, and where "it," whatever it is, is never enough.

Richard Rohr said, "Addiction is the fruit of idolatry."[66] Just as idols are often hidden, we are many times unaware of the addiction (a friendlier word may be attachment) which impairs our relationship with God and others. Like a fish not aware of the water in which it swims, we are not aware of the effects of our material culture.

Gerald May explains it this way; "...addiction is a state of compulsion, obsession, or preoccupation that *enslaves* a person's will and desire. Addiction sidetracks and eclipses the energy of our deepest, truest desire for love and goodness. We succumb because the energy of our desire becomes attached, nailed to specific behaviors, objects, or people."[67] *(emphasis added)*

Notice the word "enslaves" in the above definition (see also Romans 8:14–16). Without knowing, we can become in bondage to our materialistic culture. Our capitalistic economy is not "free." A democracy is free, one vote for one person. Capitalism gives power to the 800-pound gorilla, the individual or group who can amass the most money.[68] Seventy percent of the population is thought to have no say in public policy.[69] No longer do we serve a benevolent master. No longer can we say "no" to our *affluent* lifestyle. And life in America is *affluent* compared to the rest of the world. As St. Augustine would say, "our loves are disordered," which he defined as "sin."

The source of the bondage is often our addictions, driven by the discomfort caused by anxiety. The bondage, in turn, blocks that for which we were **created to love.**

> Love is the source and goal. Faith is the slow process of getting there. Hope is the willingness to move forward without resolution and closure. And these are indeed, "the three things that last" (1 Corinthians 13:13). People who have these gifts — faith, hope, and love — are indestructible.[70]

Normally one cannot see their own addiction by themselves. Growth and change requires community. Ironically though, community can also cause lots of trouble. We have great difficulty knowing what we can and cannot afford. All too often we look to what our neighbor is doing to make our decisions, in other words, we attempt "to keep up with the Joneses."

Tim Keller writes:

> Why can't anyone in the grip of greed see it? The counterfeit god of money uses powerful sociological and psychological dynamics. Everyone tends to live in a particular socioeconomic bracket. Once you can afford to live in a particular neighborhood, send your children to its schools, and participate in its social life, you will find yourself surrounded by quite several people who have more

> money than you. You don't compare yourself to the rest of the world, you compare yourself to those in your bracket. The human heart always wants to justify itself and this is one of the easiest ways. You say, "I don't live as well as him or her or them. My means are modest compared to theirs." You can reason and think like that no matter how lavishly you are living.[71]

Left to ourselves or looking only to our neighbor, as Keller notes above, can result in too high a standard of living that is difficult to maintain and very difficult to reduce. We get used to it (addicted maybe?) A high standard of living, just like having too much debt, can be a form of bondage. God's desire for us is to be free of bondage (Galatians 5:1).

The story of the Israelites deliverance from Egypt is a story of God releasing his people from bondage. Our attachment to things other than God, things that our materialistic culture values, is not what we were made for. True value is only in proper relationship with God.

The comfort of a high standard of living also carries with it the danger of what Killian Noe, in her book *Finding Our Way Home,* calls "ambivalence." We just do not see a reason to change.

Noe adapts the following plan (commonly used with addicted and homeless men and women) to fit those of us struggling to live in God's way of love as follows:

> **First,** get honest with ourselves and God,
>
> **Second,** we share our ambivalent feelings with another human being, and
>
> **Third,** immerse ourselves in "the community of faith, the alternative culture."[72]

Similarly, Ched Myers in his excellent article, *Beyond 'The Addict's Excuse': Sin, Public Addiction and Ecclesial Recovery,* proposes three steps to walk more in God's kingdom. He relates his steps to the 12-Step Tradition of Alcoholics Anonymous (a modification of the 12-

Steps to Sabbath Economics is included in the appendix). Myers writes:

- Acknowledge the addictive system (Step One)
- Appeal to and yield to a "Higher Power" (Steps Two and Three)
- Accept culpability in the addictive system and "confess" it to others (Steps Four and Five)
- Seek to repent of those practices (Steps Six and Seven)
- Make reparation to those wronged (Steps Eight and Nine)

Myers writes that just because the problem is overly large, which can be a source of anxiety; there is no excuse to not enter the steps above. "We must acknowledge and understand how we are part of the addictive system (complicity) and how it is a part of us (internalization). This allows us to recognize the power of the system over us (our addiction) in a way that does not concede impotence or resignation (the addict's excuse)."[73]

Likewise, we must realize that though our efforts are not going to change the problems, at least not in the near future. Our soul is dependent upon the acknowledgment of these addictions.

"The external deserts in the world are growing, because the internal deserts have become so vast."[74] It is these "...simple daily gestures which break the logic of violence, exploitation and selfishness."[75]

The Real Cost of Idolatry

If our personal addictions or sins are difficult to recognize, our culture's shortcomings, systemic sins, are maybe more difficult. We know things are not right, but really, we do not know how to make them right. Peter Drucker, noted management consultant, educator and author, is credited with saying, "Culture eats strategy for breakfast."

Even with the known problems of our materialistic culture, it is extremely difficult "to go against the grain." When others are buying the big house or the expensive cars, the simplicity of trying to follow our Lord (which is at the heart of the Gospel) is hard. The constant bombardment of the messages of our culture affects us more than I think we realize. We must ask if we want our lifestyle informed by this culture.

Tim Keller asks, "If our entire culture strongly encourages us to adopt the counterfeit god, how can we escape it?"[76]

Sabbath Economics addresses our idolatry by acknowledging the problem (through analytical, financial analysis), the commitment to specific actions, and in the presence of community. It is the *means* to accomplish a *vision* – not a vision corrupted by this world but of an Eternal source.

> If we are to grow up spiritually, if we are to become who we were created to become, we need **structures** in our lives in which we are held accountable to that becoming. We need **people in our lives** who will hold us to the commitments that keep us in the process of growing spiritually. Again, spiritual practices like prayer, sharing of resources and being with the suffering and excluded have no power in themselves to heal and transform. These practices merely keep us in the process of growing up spiritually. Spiritual practices are what keep the doors of our hearts open to the power of the Spirit of God. That Spirit does the healing and transforming.[77] (emphasis added).

Timeless instructional words for overcoming bondage and becoming free in search of the *vision*:

> If you abide in my word, you are truly my disciples, and you will know the truth, and the truth will set you free.... Truly, truly, I say to you, everyone who practices sin is a slave to sin. The slave does not remain in the house forever; the son remains forever. So, if the Son sets you free, you will be free indeed. ~ John 8: 1–36

> ... all who are led by the Spirit of God are sons of God. For you did not receive the spirit of slavery to fall back into fear, but you have received the Spirit of adoption as sons, by whom we cry, "Abba! Father!" ~ Romans 8:14 –16

Without structure or a model to live by, we can slip back into bondage. Though we relish our freedom, is it a "freedom *from*" or a "freedom *for*"? Freedom, as the world defines it, leads to addiction, to anxiety, and alienation.* As Daniel Bell writes in *The Economy of Desire*, "Bondage might be described as 'doing whatever I want,' whereas freedom might be described as doing the will of God."[78]

The Gospel frees us from having to pursue the American dream in search of dignity. In the will of God, we can find significance and find it abundantly.

It can be counterintuitive to think structure can bring freedom from bondage. However, as noted Christian leader and thinker, Os Guinness, has said, "Unfettered freedom could prove to be the Achilles' heel of the modern world, dissipating into license, triviality, corruption and a grand undermining of all authority...."[79] And Mark Reynolds suggests, "Idols arising from our underlying sin too easily can creep into our lives, creating bondage, without our knowledge and idolatry almost always leads to slavery."[80]

Structure, accompanied by community, can help prevent these idols and resulting addictions.

Earlier we recounted how the Israelites in the wilderness grumbled against Moses and God, stating they would rather live in bondage in Egypt than in the wilderness with God. He answered by giving them the daily ration of manna. However, as we see in the following passage, they could not follow God's rules and suffered the consequences:

---

*My original title for this book was *I'm Addicted, You're Addicted*. Fortunately, more intelligent minds prevailed! We are quick to say that others are addicted, but according to Gerald May in *Addiction and Grace*, we are all, to some degree, addicted to possessions, power, and human relationships. These addictions give us something to turn from to God, i.e. we repent.

> And Moses said to them, "Let no one leave any of it over till the morning." But they did not listen to Moses. Some left part of it till the morning, and it bred worms and stank. And Moses was angry with them. ~ Exodus 16:19–20

As Wilkerson outlines below, the Israelites' disobedience was the result of underlying sin (lust) that created an idol of security on their own terms:

> First, their desire wasn't simply for a daily fill of bread. That was merely a thin cover over a bottomless pit of desire to have life on their terms. They wanted bread, and they wanted it now. Gathering it a day at a time wasn't good enough; they wanted to stockpile. Taking a break from gathering to give thanks on the seventh day wouldn't do either; they wanted more and more at every opportunity. The Bible has a word for such insatiable desire: lust (e.g., Rom. 13:14; James 1:14; 1 John 2:16 NASB). Though lust usually connotes sexual desire, a lust can be any sinfully excessive desire. Like a poison ivy itch, when you scratch it, it itches even more. It's never satisfied, never grateful — it only grows. Ephesians 4:19 captures the greediness of lust with the phrase "a continual lust for more."[81] (NIV)

If indeed God desires true freedom for us, then a framework, such as Sabbath Economics, should be helpful. Is it fair to ask if we would rather be controlled by the materialistic society or follow God to a promised land?

> So, Jesus said to the Jews who had believed him, "If you abide in my word, you are truly my disciples, and you will know the truth, and the truth will set you free." They answered him, "We are offspring of Abraham and have never been enslaved to anyone. How is it that you say, 'You will become free'?"
>
> Jesus answered them, "Truly, truly, I say to you, everyone who practices sin is a slave to sin. The slave does not remain in the house forever; the son remains forever. So, if the Son sets you free, you will be free indeed. I know that you are offspring of Abraham; yet you seek to kill me because my word finds no place in you. I speak

of what I have seen with my Father, and you do what you have heard from your father." ~ John 8:31–38

We find freedom in God because of his abundance, though this is strangely a difficult reality in which to live. I continue to admit to this struggle. We have contrasted abundance with its opposite, i.e. scarcity. Our consumer culture teaches us that there is never enough, that we need to get it, and get even more. We tend to look at other people based solely on what we can gain from them. This is called capitalism and it is basically all we know.

Lynne Twist is a global activist, fundraiser, speaker, consultant, and author. I like her book *The Soul of Money* because, frankly, she comes to the issue of abundance from a secular perspective. In her book, she outlined three toxic myths that support the scarcity mindset:

Toxic Myth #1: There's Not Enough

We tend to think the Earth's resources are a "fixed pie"–there is not enough to go around. "*There's not enough generates* a fear."

Toxic Myth #2: More Is Better

"It's a logical response. If you fear there's not enough, but *more is better* drives the competitive culture of accumulation, acquisition and greed that only heightens fears and quickens the pace of the race." We act as if our self-worth is connected to our net worth.

Toxic Myth #3: That's Just the Way It Is

Operating as if the world's problems are just too big,–leads to a justification of "the greed, prejudice, and an action that scarcity fosters in our relationship with money and the rest of the human race."[82]

Like a fish not aware of the water in which it swims, it is very difficult for us to see the true reality, of which Twist further writes:

> Bernard Lietaer, former senior officer of the Belgian Central Bank and one of the chief architects of the Euro currency, in his book, Of Human Wealth, says that greed and fear of scarcity are programmed; they do not exist in nature, not even in human nature. They are built into the money system in which we swim, and we've been swimming in it so long that these shadows have become almost completely transparent to us. We have learned to consider them normal and legitimate behavior.
>
> He concludes that Adam Smith's system of economics could more accurately be described as the allocation of scarce resources through the process of individual greed. The whole process of Smith's "modern" economics actually has its roots in primitive fears of scarcity, greed, and the implementation tool – the process by which this became real – was money.[83]

Brueggemann says that scarcity fuels anxiety, resulting in an end of faith.[84] Willard's VIM model breaks down as we seek a *vision* corrupted by the world, driven by a selfish desire that corrupts *intentionality*, and using worldly tools of the Pharaoh as *means*.

Instead of futilely claiming promises that God never made, a better way seems to align with His will, to trust His goodness. Maybe this is true abundance – not riches, nor power, nor physical healing. Sabbath Economics helps you to align your life more with this will.

> I suggest that sufficiency is precise. Enough is a place you can arrive at and dwell in. So often we think of "abundance'" as the point at which we'll know we've really arrived, but abundance continues to be elusive if we think we'll find it in some excessive amount of something. True abundance does exist; it flows from sufficiency, in an experience of the beauty and wholeness of what is. Abundance is a fact of nature. It is a fundamental law of nature, that there is enough and it is finite. Its finiteness is no threat; it creates a more accurate relationship that commands respect, reverence, and managing those resources with the knowledge that they are precious and in ways that do the most good for the most people.[85]

4

The Seven Covenants of Sabbath Economics

◆ ◆ ◆

As I have attempted to show, not only are we individually corrupted, but the culture has its own hidden influences. We desire more *shalom*, a peace without anxiety. Sabbath Economics attempts to fashion a biblical vision of a way of life with enough for everyone and God's peace reigns. Ched Meyer, the creator of Sabbath Economics, developed seven household practices, or covenants, to effect this way of life. Covenant is not a word used much today, but I liked Thomas Merton's definition of the word. He defined covenant as "… saying that man is a true son of God, called to share in the work attending and using the world created by God, of participating in a work which is being carried out in history."[86]

Surplus Capital

Where your treasure is, there your heart will be also. ~ Jesus

The first covenant, or household practice, that we are going to look at concerns the money that you do not need immediately–for example retirement savings or an emergency fund. In fact, we will divide this practice under two headings:

- Retirement Savings
- Short Term Investment Savings

When you invest in a company, either by buying stock or through a mutual fund, you are becoming a small owner of that enterprise. As Christians, of course, we would not purposefully want to be in the business of making money from pornography, abortion, etc. However, we usually have no idea about the exact practices of the businesses that make up our investments.

We mentioned the term "ambivalence" in the introduction to this book. Ask yourself, "Is ambivalence okay, with regard to my investments?"

To invest only in companies which do not violate biblical principles is usually denoted as biblically responsible investing (a subset of socially responsible investing). The normal approach is to exclude from possible investment those companies which violate a specified value system (which is different for every "screen"). The standard biblically responsible investing, or BRI, reasoning is as follows:

> The way we invest not only affects our financial goals, but it affects the broader culture. When we choose to invest in any security, we become owners in a company and help support (financially) the mission and vision of that company. The dollars that we vote will either continue to reinforce and grow companies that bring true value to our world or companies that are less than valuable.[87]

Though the reasoning is sound (and it is not my intent to cast any dispersion on BRI), I just was not moved to place a large percentage of my investable resources in BRI type funds. The standard response to BRI, as articulated by Austin Pryor of *Sound Mind Investing*, is as follows:

> Our options are limited by the fact that we are "in the world" and must function in it. Paul writes in 1 Corinthians 5:9–10: "I have written you in my letter not to associate with sexually immoral people—not at all meaning the people of this world who are immoral, or the greedy and swindlers, or idolaters. In that case, you would have to leave this world."
>
> Paul recognizes the impossibility of completely avoiding all contact with disagreeable associations in the course of living our daily lives.
>
> Some people believe that it's wrong to have any money invested in objectionable companies. Even if such a standard was attainable, there is still the question of whether the incremental gain in the purity of the portfolio is worth the likely decrease in investment return. For example, I want to breathe clean air, yet I don't feel the need to walk around wearing a gas mask—at a certain point, the marginal improvement in purity isn't worth the increased restriction. Likewise, I avoid investing directly in companies whose products or policies run counter to my values, but I also don't fret that minuscule holdings of objectionable companies may temporarily pass through my fund portfolio....
>
> Ultimately, I want us to become more effective by extending our ethical concerns to all areas of stewardship—our work, our spending, our investing, and our giving. Am I saying that "if you can't do it perfectly, then don't even try?" Of course, not. I'm saying that it is helpful to make a distinction between the things you can do perfectly (or almost perfectly) and the things you cannot. Far be it from us as Christians, who are responsible for handling God's wealth for God's glory, that we should provide direct financial support to the very people and institutions whose activities are undermining the biblical values we hold dear. I believe that it's possible to almost completely avoid having direct involvement or

> lending direct support to objectionable companies. So, make it a priority to do so across the stewardship spectrum. And with respect to the things that you cannot do perfectly, such as avoiding all indirect involvement or support in your spending and investing, do what you reasonably can while keeping your stewardship responsibilities in balance.[88]

Pryor outlines how our employment and purchasing decisions have much stronger influences on a company. In addition, the "rights of ownership" have changed over the last 30 or 40 years. Though owning stocks can still be profitable, the rights of ownership have shifted more to company management and investment managers.

Lynn Stout, respected Cornell Law school professor, makes the case in her book *The Shareholder Value Myth* summarized below:

1) Neither shareholders, nor anyone else, are the legal owners of corporations and

2) U.S. law does not obligate senior management and directors to make the interests of shareholders' paramount.[89]

Whether or not individual stockholders ever had any sway with management (and Stout does say that CEOs still act as if shareholders are the beneficial owners of public corporations), it has most certainly decreased. While these points may strengthen the "non-BRI" position outlined by Mr. Pryor above, I am reminded of the work of Wendell Berry, a Kentucky farmer, writer, and sometimes theologian. Berry speaks of the loss of touch with the rhythms of God because we are no longer tied to the land. Assuming we are going to own stock positions as we attempt to save for such things as retirement, maybe we need to give more attention to be truly involved. In keeping with Jesus' statement "Where your treasure is, there your heart will be also" (Matthew 6:21), BRI can be used as a tool to take more of a stewardship interest in an investment, more connection with your money in the life that God has for you.

The more time I spend contemplating Sabbath Economics, the more convinced I become of the BRI philosophy. Though I do not think my small amount of "surplus" money will change anything, it has become a small way that I worship Christ. I trust that even a small change in my heart is valuable to God.

Short-term or Emergency Savings

A much stronger case, I think, is made with the *location* of short-term savings. Since these funds need to be readily accessible, standard investment advice is that this money be kept in such things as savings accounts or CDs.

As emphasized in Sabbath Economics, God has a preferential option for the poor. By placing funds with financial institutions that work in low income areas, your money can help provide needed capital to those shut out of the normal financial industry. Community Development Financing Institution (CDFI) is a federal designation given such entities. By opening the account with a CDFI, it is possible to get FDIC insurance, give up little to no return, and help the poor.

"CDFIs are helping families finance their first homes, supporting community residents starting businesses, and investing in local health centers, schools, or community centers. CDFIs strive to foster economic opportunity and revitalize neighborhoods."[90]

A Sample First Step

Even if you do not have a large amount of resources, you can still participate in helping the less fortunate. A little bit of effort may have to be extended if a CDFI is not in your community, but that does not mean you cannot assist. In the past, I have used North Carolina CDFI Self-Help Credit Union (https://www.self-help.org/). One can open an account on the website of this federally insured institution. Again, it is not as easy as opening a savings account at your neighborhood bank, but hopefully God honors such small steps.

Though the BRI community touts you do not give up return by investing in this manner, it seems reasonable to assume that the return on your investments will at least be lowered by the cost of the screening. Sabbath Economics calls us to question our addiction to the pursuit of money and the security that we think it brings. Unaware, we can be in bondage to our market economy. Our "need" for income, financial independence, standard of living support can be dictated more by the culture than our personal values. Likewise, our need or addiction for comfort, restrains us from keeping money where it can help the poor. As one thought leader wrote:

> Can we simply put our disposable money wherever we can reap the greatest profit at the lowest risk, which seems to be the prevailing popular notion? Is it reasonable to use our money to make more money, without careful consideration of the goals and practices of the entities that use our money? Are there alternative ways to make our money available to movements, cooperatives, and projects that help rather than exploit or bypass the poor, without necessarily losing what we may need in the future?[91]

Consideration of the other six covenants can be influential to the manner we invest. For example, the practice of **Solidarity** (specifically spending time with those outside your economic strata) brings a love for the poor while contemplating the gift of **God's Creation** creates an attitude of gratefulness and desire to protect this planet. In fact, a relatively new form of investing has developed named *Impact Investing*. Whereas the normal BRI investment "screens out" undesirable companies, *Impact Investing* attempts to invest in those companies that are making "an impact."

If allowed, an element of peace can come from your surplus capital positioned with an effort to please God. With His help, we do not have to be in bondage to the market economy.

> Let me assume the role of eternal financial counselor and offer this advice: Choose your investments carefully; compare their return; consider their ultimate trustworthiness; and especially compare how they are we working for you one million years from now. ~ Randy Alcorn[92]

Negative Capital

... the borrower is servant to the lender. ~ Proverbs 22:7 (KJV)

In a "former life," back in the '90s, I owned a company described as managing mortgages. In reality, I bought packages of defaulted loans from the FDIC. I was a debt collector. The above verse, though not very often, was all too real. A situation would develop where the borrower realized he was at my mercy. The borrower obviously did not like it and frankly I did not like it either. It made me feel all too uncomfortable.

Debt is a part of our culture, but is also the source of much pain. Larry Burkett, co-founder of Crown Financial Ministries, defines debt as, "The total of unsecured liabilities exceeds total assets (in other words, if a calamity took place, there would be a negative balance)."[93] In today's preferred way of viewing it, if you can liquidate something to retire the obligation, we will not call that debt. And it is that definition which I will try to expand on.

A lack of contentment in present circumstances is, frankly, the only explanation to incur debt. Yes, sometimes for example, a house declines in value and thus a mortgage will become a debt in the aforementioned definition. But when I use my credit card without having cash in the bank to make the payment, it is hard to make the case that I am not saying that God will not take care of me. Borrowing is a presumption on the future (James 4:14). And "... Debt is always a shift from future spending to the present."[94]

We keep going back to the account of the Israelites in the wilderness. Obviously while the Israelites were slaves in Egypt, they were in bondage. Their meals were meager and unfulfilling, but they did not have to worry about their provision. In the wilderness, the Israelites did not see a ready supply of food. They preferred the bondage of Egypt, with its source of food, to the wilderness with their God. They preferred bondage! Moses was trying to show them a better way – a way of freedom that culminated with Jesus Christ. (Galatians 5:1)

Our culture is constantly bombarding us with messages that we must possess to be significant. To possess, we must borrow. Our materialistic capitalistic system thrives on debt. When borrowing slows, economic activity is greatly reduced. Known as "the paradox of thrift,"[95] what is good for an individual (which is to save and get out of debt) is not good for the overall economy.

As Os Guinness said:

> Nothing symbolizes the magic power of the consumer revolution better than the birth of the credit card, introduced by the Bank of America in California in 1958 as the grand fulfillment of three D's: debt, desire and democracy. What the credit card has done is transform our modern assessment of value. Value is no longer estimated by the ingenuity and sweat of the labor taken to produce something, but by the degree of satisfaction it promises its purchaser.[96]

We can also become indebted to a lifestyle. One of the most insightful questions I ever had the honor of hearing was from a 30-year-old to a group of guys in their 50s. The question, "How do you stay off "the hamster wheel'?" meaning, how do you not get wrapped up in the affluent lifestyle that so many of us, me included, feel compelled to live? A sad comment: Ten years later the 30-year-old is now struggling to make the payments on a much too big house. Debt has been around as long as there has been money.[97] People have referred to debt by many names, but it is still spending that presumes upon the future (the latest popular name seems to be "leverage.")

Renowned Harvard economist, John Kenneth Galbraith, in his book, *A Short History of Financial Euphoria*, claimed there really is nothing new under the sun with respect to investments as they are just promoted differently with debt. He traced how the investment community habitually repackages debt under different names from the Holland Tulip Crisis of the 1630s to the junk bond debacle of the 1980s.[98]

Man seems always to have been attracted to the sense of control, the sense of increase without cost (which could be construed as greed), that debt provides.

Debt restricts your ability to follow your heart as God would lead, as it places you in bondage to the culture. Though nobody will admit to trying to "keep up with the Joneses," we are all affected by the society in which we live. Many who resist, unfortunately, resist from a spirit of poverty. Their frugality comes from a fear of the future as opposed to a love for God, the God of abundance. Without community, without close relationships, is very difficult to resist the lure and call for more from our culture. It is a too fine a line to walk alone.

Giving

But since you excel in everything – in faith, in speech, in knowledge, in complete earnestness and in the love, we have kindled in you – see that you also excel in this grace of giving. ~ 2 Corinthians 8:7 (NIV)

If God is the God of abundance, the owner of "the cattle on a thousand hills" (Psalm 50:10), then He does not need your money. If He wanted to feed everybody, He would feed them (remember, the manna given to the Israelites in the wilderness and Jesus with the loaves and fishes). Why He allows bad things to happen is beyond the scope of this book (and for which I am not capable of having an answer anyway.)

Why give? Or maybe, as the above verse above implies, we should be thankful for the opportunity to give, to participate in His work. Maybe giving is as much for the giver as for the recipient. As God's nature is to give (John 3:16), we who are made in his image (Genesis 1:28) need to give to live out our true nature. Medical research shows our bodies react positively to giving. As reported in the *Chicago Tribune*, "The benefits of giving are significant, [including]: lower blood pressure, lower risk of dementia, less anxiety and depression, reduced cardiovascular risk, and overall greater happiness."[99]

It is counterintuitive to think that giving can reduce anxiety. Our need, at least perceived, is so great. The world's needs are so great. A commitment to the stewardship coaching process can help with the motivation, direction, and power to walk in this way of generosity. To reiterate, concentrating on one practice can result in a false sense of pride in one's efforts.

> Every tithe of the land, whether of the seed of the land or of the fruit of the trees, is the Lord's; it is holy to the Lord. ~ Leviticus 27:30

Without a holistic view, it is easy to get hung up on theological arguments. Is tithing required in the New Testament? How much was "required" in the Old Testament? By looking at the above verse and Deuteronomy 14:23 and 28, one can make the case that the law required 23%, not just 10%. In fact, a case has been made that the tithe was only required of landowners.[100]

But I think these theological arguments miss the point. Throughout the Bible, giving is strongly reinforced. The idea that tithing is the "training wheels of giving"[101] makes sense to me. We should give, but giving should come from a love of God and others. The power is in the relationships of the covenants. Personally, as I have meditated on how the other six covenants relate with generosity, I feel like I am beginning to see a little bit of the mind or heart of God. Giving becomes more purposeful.

An early church saying, "You are to let your offering sweat in the palm of your hand until you know for whom it is intended" captures what I am trying to say.[102] Giving is obviously intended for God. By engaging in Sabbath Economics, by looking at the seven covenants holistically, a little bit of the mind of God can be seen. Giving, in and of itself, is good but not great. The years 2014 and 2015 saw a record amount of money donated.[103] And though the ratio of people in poverty is declining, the overall numbers are increasing.[104] Concentrating more on the reason for giving, instead of the actual act itself, I think will not only increase giving but also target for the most good.

Giving is not a thing I feel like I have to do, but the thing I **want** to do to participate more in His work. Hopefully more of His strength, and less of mine, is involved in the giving process.

Of course, it is still hard.

When we are honest with ourselves, we realize how addicted we are to Mammon, a term Jesus used in relation to money (Matthew 6:24). Our fear and anxiety is self-attestation of that addiction. But nothing breaks this addiction better than giving. Noted theologian Dr. Ken Boa of Reflection Ministries said, "We desecrate the altar of Mammon by giving it away."[105]

God's Creation

> In the beginning, God created the heavens and the earth.
> ~ Genesis 1:1

> And He is before all things, and in Him all things hold together.
> ~ Colossians 1:17

- The "retreat" of the glaciers evidences the warming of our climate.[106]

- The rate of disappearance of animal species evidences the possible beginning of a mass extinction.[107]
- Our increasing reliance on natural resources, specifically rare earth minerals, evidences our unsustainable economic structure.[108]

Controversy and conflict are rampant in the discussion of environmental concerns. The influence of man's activities or man's resourcefulness in solving problems is heavily debated. It is not my purpose to wade into such a morass.

> Battling about legal controls is pointless, unless we can persuade people of the human richness of a culture informed by that radical openness to meaning that is ready to leave behind the calculations of profit and public utility as the only tests of success and political viability.[109]

Everything, though, is a gift. The beauty of a sunset, a cool wind blowing across your face, a flower, or even the taste of a good cheeseburger-these can and should be opportunities to express gratitude. Care of the environment can be driven not so much by a felt need to be "green," but a sign of a love for God.

Walter Brueggeman describes our culture as a "predatory economy" and the "extraction system."[110] In his wonderfully unusual novel, *My Ishmael*, author Daniel Quinn uses the term the "takers" for what we would call "civilized."[111]

Is our treatment of the earth done with a sense of entitlement or gratitude?

With issues so large, one can feel their individual efforts do not matter. But since most environmental movements do not contain a desire to glorify God, is joining in community with these groups good? Can such efforts help to break addictions contrary to our true values? As quoted by Ched Myers in his insightful article entitled "Beyond 'The Addict's Excuse': Sin, Public Addiction and Ecclesial Recovery."

> What is wrong, says Wendell Berry plainly, is that "we all live by robbing nature, but our standard of living demands that the robbery shall continue" (1989:19). We are so internally captive to our illusions, excesses and appetites that we can no longer imagine the world differently and our little theologies of sin can't explain why. Berry, however, has this suggestion: we are using "the addict's excuse, and we know that it will not do."[112]

If climate change is a true problem, the poor of the world will bear the brunt of the effects. They could also bear the largest brunt of any efforts to curb environmental change. The problems seem so insurmountable that maybe the only true solution will be found from God working through community.

And whether or not you believe climate change is a problem, others do. The ramifications are really beyond comprehension (a recent study showed 470 to 760 million people could lose their homes due to coastal flooding associated with environmental change).[113] That a country could take desperate measures to protect themselves is not inconceivable. Some of these measures are not prohibitively expensive. For instance, climate engineering or geo-engineering can entail spraying metal particles in the upper atmosphere in an effort to reduce global temperatures. As this strategy is untested, other countries could declare war to attempt to stop the spraying (this came home to me while mistakenly watching a really, really bad movie called *Snowpiercer*). Again, global community appears crucial.

To repent, to turn away, from the predatory or extraction society can be an effort to break unseen addictions that hamper our spiritual growth. It can help to express gratitude to the One who made us and make it easier to join in the global community.

As someone raised in Texas, such environmental practices are rather foreign. But as my spirit of thankfulness grows through meditation on Sabbath Economics and its seven covenants, I am finding a growing desire to protect this gift we call earth.

The wind, one brilliant day, called
to my soul with an odor of jasmine.
'In return for the odor of my jasmine,
I'd like all the odor of your roses.'
'I have no roses; all the flowers
in my garden are dead.'
'Well then, I'll take the withered petals
and the yellow leaves and the waters of the fountain.'
The wind left. And I wept. And I said to myself:
'What have you done with the garden that was entrusted to you?'[114]

Consumption

"All spending decisions are spiritual decisions" goes a common saying. The interrelationship between the covenants is most evident in the covenant of "consumption."

Consider the following:

- ***Surplus Capital*** – obviously the more you spend the less money you will have to save. Also, you would not want to support a company with your business that you would not want to take an ownership interest (i.e. own stock).
- ***Negative Capital*** – the most prominent reason for going into debt is consumption level is too high.
- ***Generosity*** – obviously the more you spend on yourself, the less you have to give.

And it is probably a fair assumption that the more stuff you own and take care of, the less time you have to think about *God's Creation*, other people (*Solidarity*), or relax with God (*Sabbath*).

Though a reading "between the lines" would lead one to think I was talking about being on a budget, (and budgets are obviously great), the similarity is too high with the diet, and we do not diet well. Long-term, budgets only seem to work for certain people.[115]

Fortunately, as discussed earlier, you can be "seized by a new affection" – your "want to's" can change. By entering the Sabbath Economics process, even with a small physical effort but a mental commitment, you can begin to see something greater than this temporal world around us.

The Spirit must be involved because the culture's influence is so strong. As Daniel M. Bell Jr. wrote in his book, *The Economy of Desire (The Church and Postmodern Culture): Christianity and Capitalism in a Postmodern World:*

> Yet given the depth of capitalism's hold on us, the extent of its discipline in a marketized society and world, and the pilgrim or fugitive character of the divine economy, we may find ourselves at the end of this work perhaps like the blind man of Bethsaida touched once by Jesus. That is, we may catch a glimpse of a different ordering of desire, we may sense the attraction of a different economy, but things still remain so foggy. All we see are walking trees. Capital's hold is still so strong.[116]

Our culture is always telling us to consume more, but the pull of the Gospel is less, towards a simplicity of life.[117] Not simplicity for simplicity's sake, but as in the parable:

> The kingdom of heaven is like treasure hidden in a field, which a man found and covered up. Then in his **joy** he goes and sells all that he has and buys that field. ~ Matthew 13:44 [emphasis added]

Solidarity

Today, it is fashionable to talk about the poor. Unfortunately, it is not so fashionable to talk with them. ~ Mother Teresa

A typhoon stranded a monkey on an island. In a protected place on the shore, while waiting for the raging waters to recede, he spotted a fish swimming against the current. It seemed to the monkey that the fish was struggling and needed assistance. Being of kind heart, the monkey resolved to help the fish.

> A tree leaned precariously over the spot where the fish seemed to be struggling. At considerable risk to himself, the monkey moved far out on a limb, reached down, and snatched the fish from the waters. Scurrying back to the safety of the shelter, he carefully laid the fish on dry ground. For a few moments, the fish showed excitement but soon settled into a peaceful rest. ~ An Eastern parable[118]

By solidarity, we mean intentionally spending time with a different socioeconomic class, i.e. usually the poor. One of the reasons, I think, for God's "preferential option for the poor" is that they have much to teach us. Without spending time in another's world, we can, like the monkey in the story, have good intentions but horrible results. The movie *Poverty, Inc.* is a stark testimony to this fact.[119]

We spend so much time in our own little circle trying to survive, trying to get ahead, trying to juggle all the balls we have in the air, it sometimes takes breaking out of that mode and putting yourself in a different situation to see reality.

Consider the "advantages" to being poor:

1. The poor know they are in urgent need of redemption.
2. The poor know not only their dependence on God and on powerful people, but also their interdependence with one another.
3. The poor rest their security not on things but on people.
4. The poor have no exaggerated sense of their own importance, and no exaggerated need of privacy.
5. The poor expect little from competition and much from cooperation.
6. The poor can distinguish between necessities and luxuries.
7. The poor can wait, because they have acquired a kind of dogged patience born of acknowledged dependence.
8. The fears of the poor are more realistic and less exaggerated, because they already know that one can survive great suffering and want.

9. When the poor have the Gospel preached to them, it sounds like good news and not like a threat or a scolding.
10. The poor can respond to the call of the Gospel with a certain abandonment and uncomplicated totality because they have so little to lose and are ready for anything.[120]

We have become so addicted to our stuff, our comfort, our perceived security. As income inequality continues to grow in the United States, the ability to understand, to love "the unprotected"[121] becomes so much more difficult (and we just may find ourselves included in that classification!) Again, as Walter Brueggemann said, "I do not mind dying for Christ; I am ready to do that. But I do not want to be inconvenienced."[122]

I'm sure that it is evident that this covenant weighs most heavily on my heart. Ched Meyer once told me. "You are too white. " Since he is also a white Anglo-Saxon male, I do not think he meant to be disparaging. It is just hard for us to see the world through somebody else's eyes.

I do not yet know how I will live out this covenant. I am trying various activities to see where God would lead. In pursuing solidarity, my difficulties in the Sabbath covenant (slowing down instead of always trying to make money) and consumption covenant (owning to impress others) have been brought to my attention. I continually encounter my addictions and these addictions hamper and block my ability to love. May God have mercy...

And if that love should count you worthy
And should deign one day to seek your door and be your guest-
Pause ere you draw the bolt and bid him rest, if it your old content you would remain.
For not alone he enters.
In his train are children of the mist, the lonely guest, dreams of the unfulfilled in and unpossessed, and sorrow, and life's immemorial pain.
He wakes desires you never may forget.

> He shows you stars you never saw before.
> He makes you share with him forevermore the burden of the world's divine regret.
> How wise you were to open not.
> In yet, how poor, if you should turn him from the door. ~ Unknown poet[123]

Work and Sabbath

Of the seven, this is probably the hardest for me to observe. A cessation of work on Sunday is painful. I so much want to rely on my own strength.

We are too busy. It took basically 80 years to get the 40-hour workweek established and smart phones undid that in six. For the first time in history, we can work seven days a week, 24 hours a day. In my world, things move very, very fast. If not at work, I seem to have to amuse myself.

In 1985, Neal Postman wrote the book, *Amusing Ourselves to Death*. How prophetic his words:

> Social media creates a world... where a) what everyone else is doing is very out in the open, b) most people present an inflated version of their own existence, and c) the people who chime in the most about their careers are usually those whose careers (or relationships) are going the best, while struggling people tend not to broadcast their situation. This leaves [one] feeling, incorrectly, like everyone else is doing really well, only adding to [their] misery.[124]

With the decline in social activities, work has become more a source of identity, community and purpose. Yet this is not the world as God designed it. He gave us the Sabbath for a reason. For example, Pharaoh's Egypt did not have a Sabbath. The Israelites worked seven days a week. God, in his abundance, promised to take care of us with only six days of work. Thus, one of the central tenets of Sabbath Economics, there is enough for everyone.[125]

Work can become an addiction and thus create anxiety.[126] The Sabbath gives us more time to worship and minister to those around us (thus related to *Solidarity* and *God's Creation*). Without Sabbath, it is difficult for us to think critically.[127]

And maybe most importantly, the Sabbath reminds us that we are Christians with a loving God.

As Dr. Brueggeman wrote:

> Sabbath is the thing that keeps the faithful mindful of the fact that they are Jews or Christians. When we cease to be mindful that we are Jews/Christians, then we are no longer Jews/Christians. It is important to be mindful in a mindless society. Sabbath is the most important practice that we observe. Sabbath keeps us free from the anxiety over never having enough–an anxiety that continues to run rampant through our society. Sabbath frees us to take care of self and neighbor. Sabbath is God's great gift to us.[128]

I confess, I am addicted to work and I am addicted to my own efforts. Since those are obviously lacking, I am anxious. The Lord has promised to provide. Someday I hope to be able to rest in that.

Conclusion

◆ ◆ ◆

We are all attached to various things that we think will give us life or free us from the pain caused by the hole that is deep inside all of us. These attachments, these addictions, are anxiously pursued to fill in this hole but never do. These attachments and addictions, being controlled by false idols, prevent us from loving others and trapped in anxiety. As Peter Rollins said, "There is another, more radical form of freedom hinted at in the Gospels – not the freedom to pursue what we believe will satisfy us, but the freedom from the pursuit of what we believe will satisfy us."[129]

These attachments are so hard to see and impair our *vision*. We need community (Matthew 7:1–5) to encourage and support our *intentions*. And I think we need spiritual disciplines or *means* that will help us to see true reality. I believe Sabbath Economics contains those disciplines.

The desire for certainty drives so many addictions. We fear uncertainty. In the 1989 movie *Parenthood,* Steve Martin plays a neurotic father of three, whose oldest son has inherited his dad's neurotic tendencies, while the youngest likes to butt things with his head. In the final scene, Martin has just quit his job when his wife gives him the unexpected news that a fourth child is on the way. Following is a portion of the movie's script:

> [Gil, played by Steve Martin, has been complaining about his complicated life; Grandma wanders into the room]
>
> Grandma: You know, when I was nineteen, Grandpa took me on a roller coaster.

> Gil: Oh?
>
> Grandma: Up, down, up, down. Oh, what a ride!
>
> Gil: What a great story.
>
> Grandma: I always wanted to go again. You know, it was just so interesting to me that a ride could make me so frightened, so scared, so sick, so excited, and so thrilled all together! Some didn't like it. They went on the merry-go-round. That just goes around. Nothing. I like the roller coaster. You get more out of it.[130]

After the above exchange, in a particularly chaotic moment in the house, Martin begins to hear the sound of a roller coaster in his head. At first, he appears frightened. But then a smile comes to his face, and you can tell he is *enjoying* the ride. Gil is learning to embrace the anxiety that is preventing him from pursuing his *vision*.

Hebrews 11:6 says, "And without faith it is impossible to please him...." Having faith in God, as opposed to our misguided and futile efforts to run our lives as we see fit is so, so hard. Personally, I find myself white-knuckled on the roller coaster of life all too often. Rarely am I able to see past my addictions to the exciting life God has for me. Sabbath Economics helps see the *vision* and gives the *means*. Faith supplies the *intention*.

> The bottom line (and by this, I mean that we keep coming back to it over and over again) is that Love beckons us,
>
> Come to me all you who labor and are burdened and I will give you rest.
>
> When we know that Every Living Thing is lurching, groaning towards justice, then we can relax and rest. We can take Sabbath. A grace that overcomes our hypocrisies and incongruities justifies our strange experiments of Living In The Tension. And, rest assured, if we forget all of this, in moments of distraction or distortion, we *will* be forgiven.[131]

For more resources, please visit our website at
http://www.wfrplanning.com

Appendix A
12 Steps of Sabbath Economics

We are human.
We are, too often, too busy.
We are bombarded by so much information.
We are vulnerable to taking lifestyle cues from unintended sources.
We are influenced by, and often unknowingly addicted to, popular culture matters.

For over 80 years, the 12-step method of *Alcoholics Anonymous* has proven to be a successful practice for men and women to meet, and overcome, the many difficulties of life. With this in mind, the following adaptation was created to help you begin the reordering of your desires, bringing these more in line with your true nature, for living a more abundant life.

The Twelve Transformational Steps

- We admitted we were powerless over our *materialistic culture* - that our lives have become unmanageable.
- We came to believe that Jesus Christ could restore us to sanity.
- We made the decision to turn our whole lives over to the care of God in His abundance.
- We made a searching and fearless and moral inventory of ourselves especially our *consumption* habits.

- We admitted to God, to ourselves, and another human being (including entering solidarity with those less fortunate) the exact nature of our wrongs.
- We were entirely ready to have God remove these defects from our character.
- We humbly asked him to remove our shortcomings.
- We made a list of those harmed by our consumptive habits and realized the harm done by those who have preceded us.
- We made direct amends to such people whenever possible, except when to do so would injure them or others.
- We continued to take personal inventory and when we were wrong promptly admitted it.
- We sought through prayer and meditation to improve our conscious contact with God, praying only for knowledge of His will for us and the power to carry that out.

Having had a spiritual experience as a result of following this *covenant,* we tried to carry this message to others, and practice these principles in all our affairs.

◆ ◆ ◆

The great obstacle is simply this: the conviction that we cannot change
because we are dependent upon what is wrong.
But that is the addict's excuse, and we know that it will not do.
~Wendell Berry

Appendix B
Self-Discovery

The process of self-discovery can be ugly. Inside each of us are things that we would just as soon not see. Nevertheless, hiding them does not change their effect on us. By bringing them to the light the Holy Spirit, through community, can mold us more to an anxiety-free life that God made for us.

One of the most influential books for me is *The Cure* (formally called *Trueface*).[132] Using an analogy of two rooms, the authors illustrate a profound truth. They label the first room the "Room of Good Intentions." We spend most of our time in and around this room. A place where we operate behind masks, acting as if everything is "fine." Dallas Willard defines this as "sin management."[133] We work on our sin individually in a futile attempt to *please* God.

The second room goes by the name of "Room of Grace." It is in this room, the authors write and hang a banner that says: **Standing with God, my sin in front of us, working on it together.**[134] Since God "knows the number of hairs on our head" (Luke 12:7), He knows where we come up short. I think this is important to Sabbath Economics in that the seven covenants are a lifelong process. Not to get too mystical, but if this teaching is truly God pleasing, one would expect to run into spiritual warfare. When we fail, and we will, our flesh will have a tendency to concentrate on one covenant, "to do it better."

Using *The Cure* analogy, "doing it better" will move you back to the "Room of Good Intentions." This room has a comfort for us in that we are doing something, as opposed to somebody doing something through us. In writing this book, I found myself continuously slipping back into the "Room of Good Intentions." In *The Cure*, the road to each of these rooms is long, but the path between is short. For me, a voice in my head shouted "Fraud!" I believed everything I was writing in this book, but I do it so poorly.

In fact, I found myself, as *The Cure* authors describe, as being outside the "Room of Good Intentions." They wrote:

> The Room of Good Intentions broke and jaded their hearts, robbing them of hope. It made them so sick they're nearly anesthetized to believing life can ever be different. Man-made religion has beaten them down. Many are oozing with apathy. They can think of no good reason to try, they simply don't care. Some of God's most passionate, gifted, and dedicated servants are despondent along that road. These wounded express themselves in many forms. Some are cynical and smug, but it's a cover. They're self-protecting from vulnerability. They're still articulate and insightful – they just now speak from the fringes of the arena. They're bleeding from having risked vulnerability in a community that didn't know what to do with it.[135]

One of the taglines for my business is "Helping people lead God-pleasing lives...." The tagline is probably not accurate. "And without faith it is impossible to please God..." (Hebrews 11:6). Trust is the goal. Trust in disciplines such as Sabbath Economics, trust in the Bible, trust in God. A pleased God is the goal, but it is a byproduct of trust. The byproduct is the abundant life.

Appendix C

Breathing Underwater

I built my house by the sea.
Not on the sands, mind you;
not on the shifting sand.
And I built it of rock.
A strong house
by a strong sea.
And we got well acquainted, the sea and I.
Good neighbors.
Not that we spoke much.
We met in silences.
Respectful, keeping our distance,
but looking our thoughts across the fence of sand.
Always, the fence of sand our barrier,
always, the sand between.

And then one day,
– and I still don't know how it happened –
the sea came.
Without warning.

Without welcome, even.
Not sudden and swift, but a shifting across the sand like wine,
less like the flow of water than the flow of blood.
Slow, but coming.

Slow, but flowing like an open wound.
And I thought of flight and I thought of drowning and I thought of death.
And while I thought the sea crept higher, till it reached my door.
And I knew, then, there was neither flight, nor death, nor drowning.
That when the sea comes calling, you stop being neighbors,
Well acquainted, friendly-at-a-distance neighbors,
And you give your house for a coral castle,

And you learn to breathe underwater.

~ Sr. Carol Bieleck, RSCJ from an unpublished work, as narrated in a short film found at http://www.relevantmagazine.com/rtv/shorts/breathing-underwater (accessed 12/17/16)

Appendix D
More Discussion on VIM

To further explain the VIM model the following is another parable by Peter Rollins.

> There was once a world-renowned philosopher who, from an early age, set himself the task of proving once and for all the nonexistence of God. Of course, such a task was immense, for the various arguments for and against the existence of God had done battle over the ages without either being able to claim victory. He was, however, a genius without equal, and he possessed a singular vision that drove him to work each day and long into every night; in order to understand the intricacies of every debate, every discussion, and every significant work on the subject.
>
> The philosopher's project began to earn him respect among his fellow professors when, as a young man, he published the first volume of what would turn out to be a finely honed, painstakingly researched, encyclopedic masterpiece on the subject of God. The first volume of this work argued persuasively that the various ideas of God that had been expressed throughout antiquity were philosophically incoherent and logically flawed. As each new volume appeared, he offered, time and again, devastating critiques of the theological ideas that had been propagated through different periods of history. In his early forties, he completed the last volume, which brought him up to the present day.
>
> However, the completion of this work did not satisfy him. He still had not found a convincing argument that would demonstrate once and for all the nonexistence of God. For all he had shown was that all the notions of God up to that time had been problematic.
>
> So, he spent another sixteen years researching arguments and interrogating them with a highly nuanced, logical analysis. But by now he was in his late fifties and had slowly begun to despair of

> ever completing his life project.
>
> Then, late one evening while he was locked away in his study, bent wearily over his old oak desk, surrounded by a vast sea of books, he felt a deep stillness descend upon the room. As he sat there motionless, everything around him seemed to radiate an inexpressible light and warmth. Then, deep in his heart he heard the voice of God address him:
>
> "Dear friend, the task you have set yourself is a futile one. I have watched all these years as you poured your being into this endless task. Yet, you fail to understand that your project can be brought to completion only with my help. Your dedication and single-mindedness have not gone unnoticed, and they have won my respect. As a result, I will tell you a sacred secret meant only for a few... Dear friend, *I do not exist.*"
>
> Then, suddenly, everything appeared as it was before, and the philosopher was left sitting at his desk with a deep smile breaking across his face. He put his pen away and left his study, never to return. Instead, in gratitude to God for helping him complete his lifelong project, he dedicated his remaining years to serving the poor.[136]

The atheist in the story did not need God to tell him what to do. We intuitively generally know how to act, the *means*. Sabbath Economics gives us a framework and a model to think about these *means*. And it gives us a way that we can look to God for *vision* and *intentionality* to give us power for our walk and not let our "righteous deeds [become] like a polluted garment" (Isaiah 64:6). For most, one just needs to begin to move. As Mississippi Fred McDowell wrote in his song "You Gotta Move."[137]

> But when the Lord
> Gets ready
> You gotta move.

Notes

◆ ◆ ◆

[1] http://www.merriam-webster.com/dictionary/repent

[2] David Leonhardt "The American Dream, Quantified at Last," http://www.nytimes.com/2016/12/08/opinion/the-american-dream-quantified-at-last.html, (accessed 12/17/16)

[3]Rollins, Peter. *The Idolatry of God: Breaking Our Addiction to Certainty and Satisfaction* (pp. 95-96). Howard Books. Kindle Edition. See also YouTube video at https://youtu.be/LVWMZ9QT6uY

[4]https://en.wikipedia.org/wiki/Telos_(philosophy)

[5] http://christinyou.net/pages/creattele.html

[6] Tommy Airey, "Adventures in Recovering the Telos ", https://radicaldiscipleship.net/2016/08/31/adventures-in-recovering-the-telos/

[7] Hesset, Paul, Christ in the End of Meaning:The Theology of Passion, page 98 & 100

[8] Walter Brueggeman, *Journey to the Common Good*, page 7

[9] Dr. Bruce Wauchope, "The Gospel and Mental Health," https://vimeo.com/35445039 (accessed 12/27/16) "

[10] Dallas Willard, Renovation of the Heart: Putting on the Character of Christ

[11] Proverbs 29:18 KJV

[12] http://www.goodreads.com/author/quotes/19982.Frederick_Buechner (accessed 12/2/16)

[13] http://www.npr.org/templates/transcript/transcript.php?storyId=97998654 (accessed 12/7/16)

[14] Fr. Richard Rohr, OFM, "Nature as a Mirror of God," (https://cac.org/nature-mirror-god-2016-11-08/, accessed 12/23/16)

[15] Daniel M. Bell, Jr., *The Economy of Desire: Christianity and Capitalism in a Postmodern World*, Kindle edition, location 1974

[16] Jon Levine, Matt Morris, Joy Williams, Rachel Platten, Matthew B. Morris, Jack Antonoff, "Stand by You," http://www.azlyrics.com/lyrics/rachelplatten/standbyyou.html, (accessed 1/23/17)

[17] John D. Caputo, *The Weakness of God: A Theology of the Event*, page 250

[18] Joe Pinsker, "Why So Many Smart People Aren't Happy," *The Atlantic*, Apr 26, 2016

[19] Thomas Merton, in a letter to Jim Forest dated February 21, 1966, reproduced in *The Hidden Ground of Love: Letters* by Thomas Merton

[20] Jan Johnson "Intentionality of the Heart," Real Change: What 12-Step Has to Say about Transformation (and why we should care), Summer 2010, www.janjohnson.org/pdf/12_step_Conversations_Course.pdf, (accessed 3/29/17)

[21] K. Killian Noe, *Finding Our Way Home: Addictions and Divine Love*

[22] Thomas Chalmers, *The Expulsive Power of a New Affection*

[23] Fr. Richard Rohr, http://www.goodreads.com/quotes/72816-we-do-not-think-ourselves-into-new-ways-of-living, (accessed 3/29/17)

[24] Nassim Taleb, *Antifragile: Things That Gain from Disorder*, Kindle edition, location 6358

[25] Richard Rohr, *The Divine Dance: The Trinity and Your Transformation,* Kindle edition, location 1887

[26] https://en.wikipedia.org/wiki/The_unexamined_life_is_not_worth_living (accessed 3/29/17)

[27] Dr. David G Benner, "Ultimate Value," http://www.drdavidgbenner.ca/transformational-knowing2/, (accessed 3/1/17)

[28] http://matrix.wikia.com/wiki/Redpill (accessed 12/16/16)

[29] http://matrix.wikia.com/wiki/Redpill (accessed 12/16/16)

[30] Barry Taylor, Radical Theology Session 3, Homebrewed Christianity

[31] Barry Taylor, *Spiritual Growth* and M Scott Peck's *Stages*

[32] http://www.merriam-webster.com/dictionary/stewardship

[33] John C. Haughey S.J, *Virtue and Affluence: The Challenge of Wealth*

[34] St. John of the Cross, Thomas Dubay, S.M., *Fire Within*, Kindle edition, Location 6021

[35] Richard Lowery, http://www.centerforfaithandgiving.org/StudyResources/StewardshipintheFirstTestamentSabbathDelight/tabid/1054/Default.aspx

[36] Ched Myers, *Biblical Vision of Sabbath Economics*

[37] Daniel Bell, *The Economy of Desire*, Kindle edition, location 2790

[38] Raj Raghunathan, *If You're So Smart, Why Aren't You Happy?*

[39] Dr. Richard Swenson, M.D., *Contentment*

[40] https://www.goodreads.com/work/quotes/48892252-highest-duty-my-search-for-what-really-matters

[41]Jeffrey Bilbro, "Puritans and The Pope: The Conflicted Christian History of American Ecological Ethics," *Front Porch Republic*, (July 6, 2015) http://www.frontporchrepublic.com/2015/07/puritans-and-the-pope-the-conflicted-christian-history-of-american-ecological-ethics/, (accessed 3/29/17)

[42]Stanley Hauerwas, "Why Community Is Dangerous," http://www.plough.com/en/topics/community/church-community/why-community-is-dangerous, (accessed 3/29/17)

[43] Dwight Edwards, *Revolution Within*, June 2016

[44] Anne Lamott, https://m.facebook.com/AnneLamott/posts/894203970709247 (accessed 7/16/2016)

[45] Julie Beck, "The Personality Trait That Fuels Anxiety," *The Atlantic*, March 18, 2015

[46] Bill Plotkin as quoted by Richard Rohr in *Emotional Sobriety: Rewiring our Programs for "Happiness"*

[47] William R. Miller, PhD, "The Prison of Privilege." Paper can be found at: http://faithandmoneynetwork.org/resources/recommended-reading/, (accessed 6/29/17)

[48] Carl Richards, "Explaining Financial Security to Clients", *Investment News*, June 20, 2016

[49] Wilkerson, Mike. *Redemption: Freed by Jesus from the Idols We Worship and the Wounds We Carry*, Kindle Edition page 112

[50] Dorothy Greco, "Fear Doesn't Have to Control You," relevantmagazine.com, January 30, 2014

[51] Stanley Hauerwas, "Why Community Is Dangerous," http://www.plough.com/en/topics/community/church-community/why-community-is-dangerous, (accessed 3/29/17)

[52] Dr. Larry Crabb, "What is Anxiety," https://youtu.be/hG4cL3cON3s (accessed 7/19/2016.)

[53] Dr. Larry Crabb, "Anxious? Go Deeper" http://www.lifeway.com/Article/Anxious-go-deeper (accessed 7/19/2016.)

[54] John Haughey, *The Holy Use of Money*

[55] Anne Case and Angus Deaton, "Rising Morbidity and Mortality in Midlife among White Non-Hispanic Americans in 21st Century," Woodrow Wilson School of Public and International Affairs and Department of Economics, Princeton University, September 17, 2015

[56] Oswald Chambers, *The Shadow of an Agony*

[57] Stanley Hauerwas [2009] "America's God" (part 1), https://youtu.be/X4a5Z4SdUss (accessed 7/16/16)

[58] Gerald G May, M.D. *Addiction and Grace*, page 3

[59] Ibid. page 28

[60] Norman Wirzba, From Nature to Creation, Kindle edition, page 48

[61] Ibid., page 83

[62] Dwight Edwards, "The Overlooked Root of Sin", The Revolution Within

[63] Bastiate, Frederick, *Economic Sophisms*

[64] http://www.wisdomquotes.com/quote/martin-luther-king-jr-8.html, (accessed 7/21/2016)

[65] Bell, location 89

[66] Addiction Vs. Idolatry http://www.sermonindex.net/modules/newbb/viewtopic.php?topic_id=4955&forum=35 (accessed 5/31/16)

[67] May, page 13

[68] Harry Dent, interview on Real Vision, February 28, 2016. See also movie *Requiem for the American Dream*

[69] Requiem for the American Dream (1:02 mark)

[70] Father Richard Rohr, https://cac.org/scripture-week-1-summary-2016-02-27/ (accessed 2/26/16)

[71]Tim Keller, *Counterfeit Gods*, Kindle edition, page 52

[72] Killian Noe, *Finding Our Way Home*

[73] Ched Myers, *Beyond 'The Addict's Excuse': Sin, Public Addiction and Ecclesial Recovery*

[74] Pope Benedict the 16th, as quoted by Pope Francis in *will*

[75] Ibid.

[76] Keller page 80

[77] Killian Noe, *Finding Our Way Home*

[78] Bell, location 2516

[79] Os Guinness, *A Free People's Suicide: Sustainable Freedom and The American Future*, page 18

[80] Mark Reynolds, Idolatry, Attachment, Addiction, and the Church (Addictions Prevention Conference 2013), https://youtu.be/pSELsY20oEc, 6:09 minute mark (accessed 7/22/16)

[81] Wilkerson, page 108

[82] Lynne Twist, *The Soul of Money: Transforming Your Relationship with Money and Life*

[83] Ibid.

[84] Grace Matters podcast, http://media.elca.org/gracematters/gm070107.mp3, (accessed 6/28/16)

[85] Twist, page 86

[86] Thomas Merton OCSO, *Thomas Merton: Opening the Bible*

[87] John Kenneth Galbraith, A Short History of Financial Euphoria

[88] Austin Pryor, "Socially Responsible Investing: The Debate Over Where to Draw the Line, *Sound Mind Investing,* https://www.soundmindinvesting.com/articles/view/socially-responsible-investing-the-debate-over-where-to-draw-the-line, (accessed 3/29/17)

[89] Lynne Stout, The Shareholder Value Myth (2012)

[90] https://www.cdfifund.gov/Documents/CDFI_infographic_v08A.pdf

[91] Ross and Gloria Kinsler, "Moral Questions about Investing and Oikocredit's Answers," http://www.jubilee-economics.org/journal/2013/7/22/moral-questions-about-investing-and-oikocredits-answers.html, (accessed 3/29/17)

[92] "The Eternal Dimension of Generosity," https://www.biblegateway.com/devotionals/stewardship-bible/4192/12/08?interface=print, (accessed 3/29/17)

[93] Larry Burkett, *How to Manage Your Money*

[94] Burkett

[95] https://en.wikipedia.org/wiki/Paradox_of_thrift

[96] Guinness, page 157

[97] David Graeber, *Updated and Expanded: The First 5000 Years*

[98] Galbraith

[99] Terri Yablonsky Stat, "Be Generous: It's A Simple Way to Stay Healthier," http://www.chicagotribune.com/lifestyles/health/sc-hlth-0812-joy-of-giving-20150806-story.html, (accessed 7/23/16)

[100] John Kelly, "The Tithe: Land Rent To God, Religion And Liberty," Acton Institute, http://www.acton.org/pub/religion-liberty/volume-14-number-4/tithe-land-rent-god, (accessed 7/25/16)

[101] Randy Alcorn, *Money Possessions and Eternity*

[102] "The Didache," http://www.earlychristianwritings.com/text/didache-roberts.html, (accessed 2/17/17)

[103] Eleanor Goldberg, "Americans Gave Record $373.25 Billion To Charity Last Year," http://www.huffingtonpost.com/entry/americans-gave-record-37325-billion-to-charity-last-year_us_5762bf3ce4b09c926cfe6158?section=, accessed 7/25/16

[104] http://therules.org/campaign/the-story-of-poverty/, accessed 7/24/16

[105] Dr. Ken Boa, "The Spiritual Disciplines of Lifestyle," https://kingdomadvisors.com/resources/the-spiritual-disciplines-of-lifestyle, accessed 7/25/16

[106] https://en.wikipedia.org/wiki/Retreat_of_glaciers_since_1850, (accessed 2/27/17)

[107] http://advances.sciencemag.org/content/1/5/e1400253, (accessed 2/27/17)

[108] http://www.cbsnews.com/news/rare-earth-elements-not-so-rare-after-all/ (accessed 2/27/17)

[109] Rowan Williams, "Embracing Our Limits, The Lessons of Laudato Si'," Commonweal,September 23, 2015, https://www.commonwealmagazine.org/embracing-our-limits, (accessed 3/29/17)

[110] Dr. Walter Brueggemann, *Walter Brueggemann: Reading the Bible Faithfully in a Predatory Economy*, https://www.youtube.com/watch?v=b4DjKcN0OZc, (accessed 7/23/16)

[111] Daniel Quinn, *My Ishmael*

[112] Ched Myers, *Beyond 'The Addict's Excuse': Sin, Public Addiction and Ecclesial Recovery*

[113] New Report and Maps: Rising Seas Threaten Land Home to Half a Billion, http://sealevel.climatecentral.org/news/global-mapping-choices, (accessed 7/23/16)

[114] Antonio Machado, *The Wind, One Brilliant Day*

[115] Richard Truitt, *Budgets and Confessions*, http://www.wfrplanning.com/budgets-and-confessions, (accessed 7/26/16)

[116] Bell, Kindle edition, location 3314

[117] John C. Haughey, The Holy Use of Money

[118] Gibbons, Dave, *The Monkey and the Fish: Liquid Leadership for a Third Culture Church*, Kindle edition, location 173

[119] *Poverty, Inc.*, http://www.povertyinc.org/.

[120] Monika Hellwig as quoted by Philip Yancey, *The Jesus I Never Knew*, page 115

[121] Peggy Noonan, "Trump and the Rise of the Unprotected" http://www.peggynoonan.com/trump-and-the-rise-of-the-unprotected/, (accessed 7/26/16)

[122] Dr. Walter Brueggemann, "Walter Brueggemann: Reading the Bible Faithfully in a Predatory Economy," https://www.youtube.com/watch?v=b4DjKcN0OZc, (accessed 7/23/16)

[123] Bill Lane Doulos, *The Radical Disciple*, page 73

[124] Neal Postman, *Amusing Ourselves to Death*

[125] Ched Myers, *Biblical Vision of Sabbath Economics*

[126] Cecilie Schou Andreassen, et al, "The Relationships between Workaholism and Symptoms of Psychiatric Disorders: A Large-Scale Cross-Sectional Study," http://journals.plos.org/plosone/article?id=10.1371/journal.pone.0152978 (accessed 7/26/16)

[127] Walter Brueggemann: "Reading the Bible Faithfully in a Predatory Economy," https://www.youtube.com/watch?v=b4DjKcN0OZc, (accessed 7/26/16)

[128] Walter Brueggemann, "Sabbath as Means of Transition from Anxious Scarcity to Grateful Abundance," http://www.salemlutheranva.org/htdocs/pastor/1204-pastor-message.pdf, (accessed 7/26/16)

[129] Peter Rollins, The Idolatry of God: Breaking Our Addiction to Certainty and Satisfaction, Kindle edition, page 80

[130] http://www.imdb.com/character/ch0015098/quotes, (accessed 3/30/17)

[131] Tommy Airey, "Living in the Tension," February 10, 2016, https://radicaldiscipleship.net/2016/02/10/living-in-the-tension/ (accessed 7/26/16)

[132] http://www.trueface.org

[133] Dallas Willard, *The Divine Conspiracy*, page 45

[134] Bruce McNicol, Bill Thrall, John Lynch, *The Cure*, Kindle edition, location 258

[135] Ibid.

[136] Pete Rollins, *The Orthodox Heretic*

[137] http://www.lyricsfreak.com/m/mississippi+fred+mcdowell/you+gotta+move_10181613.html, (accessed 2/4/17)

67872140R00053

Made in the USA
Lexington, KY
24 September 2017